THE
True and Lively
WORD

By James T. Cleland

PROFESSOR OF PREACHING
IN THE DIVINITY SCHOOL OF DUKE UNIVERSITY
AND PREACHER TO THE UNIVERSITY

CHARLES   SCRIBNER'S   SONS
NEW   YORK
1954

Foreword

In February, 1953, the Episcopal Theological School in Cambridge, Massachusetts, honored me by listening to these lectures, the first to be delivered on the Frederic Rogers Kellogg Lectureship, established by his son, The Reverend Frederic B. Kellogg, Chaplain to the Episcopal students at Harvard University. I thank the donor and the Dean, Faculty, Students and Alumni of E. T. S. for their generous welcome to me and to what I had to say.

I have sought to outline in these lectures what I think preaching is all about: its starting point; its content; its setting; its exponent; its outcome. To tackle so much in so little space is ridiculous, I know. (Chapter IV should have been expanded into two chapters!) But this is what I was asked to do; so I did it.

I have left the material in the format in which it was delivered except for the substitution of "chapter" for "lecture." It was written to be spoken rather than to be read. The original title of the series was "Words and the Word," and the chapter headings are in accordance with that designation. However, the Dean suggested that it sounded like a study in semantics and two other friends independently proposed the title now used, inspired by a petition from the prayer for the whole state of Christ's Church in the Order for the Administration of the Lord's Supper, from *The Book of Common Prayer*. It seems to me a wee bit pretentious, and I accept it only because of the whimsical comment that the lectures seemed to be true and certainly were lively. They are offered as an ecumenical gesture, delivered to Episcopalians by a Presbyterian who works for Methodists.

I am beholden to other folk, in addition to the Kelloggs, father and son. I take this chance to thank my wife whose faith encourages my work, the Reverend John Carlton who typed the manuscript as a labor of love, Mrs. Ray C. Petry who did more proofreading than I, and the Taylor family who made me at home during the lectures without fuss or bother.

In most of the Biblical quotations throughout the book I have used the *Revised Standard Version of the Bible,* copyrighted 1946 anod 1952 by the Division of Christian Education, National Council of Churches, and I acknowledge its permission to do so.

J. T. C.

Contents

I

The Words of the Bible

IT was in 1949 that I first made up my mind to write an article or a series of lectures on the subject "Words and the Word." The primer for my decision was a definition of the sermon given by Bernard Manning: A sermon is "a manifestation of the Incarnate Word, from the Written Word, by the spoken word." [1] That phrase so intrigued me that I jotted it down on a sheet of paper, and it has been staring at me from my desk for three years. This book has given me the opportunity to tell you what kind of ruminating it has made me do. The chapters which follow are not an expansion of the definition; they are not in complete accord with the definition. But it was Manning's suggestive play on the meaning of "Word" which started me on this interpretation of preaching.

There is one presupposition which will have to be

[1] Quoted in W. E. Sangster, *The Craft of Sermon Construction* (Philadelphia: The Westminster Press, 1949), p. 22.

accepted if we are to speak and hear the same language in these five chapters. It may be stated in a single sentence: Our Christian faith is a religion of revelation whose origins have been preserved for us in the pages of the Bible. That statement I do not have the time to defend; it is, however, axiomatic for all I have to say. Insofar as we are in the historic tradition of the Reformation, it is basic for our denominations. It is the burden of the first chapter of the Westminster Confession of Faith. It underlies Articles VI and VII of the Thirty-nine Articles of Religion of the Protestant Episcopal Church in the United States of America, and is preserved in Articles V and VI by the Methodist Church. That presupposition must be kept in mind, though it will have to be interpreted.

How, then, did my reflections take form? They were chaotic to start with, but in time a pattern began to emerge. Bit by bit, with groanings oft and travail of spirit, they took shape. I started with the Bible as the source book of the revelation, and the first two chapters deal with it.

*   *   *   *   *   *

On July 8, 1918, my birthday, my mother gave me a Bible. She had written on the fly leaf this verse: "Commit thy way unto the Lord; trust also in him; and he shall bring it to pass" (Psalm 37:5). She verbally added the comment: "When the King was a small boy he promised his mother that he would read one chapter of the Bible every night. He has kept that promise. If the King could do that for his mother, it is surely not too much to expect that one of his subjects will do as much for his mother." So I began to partake of the Scriptures with regularity, one dose per night as directed. The first four chapters of Genesis intrigued me: the story of creation, the stupidity of Adam and Eve, and a good murder. Chapter five wearied me as the writer began the "begats," a forerunner of much, recurrent boredom. But Genesis rallied quickly, and through Exodus the nightly chapter, read in bed after I had said my prayers, wasn't too much of a chore. However, you can realize what Leviticus and Numbers, parts of Chronicles, and Ezra did to me. I was too young to know what to make of Job and Ecclesiastes and the Song of Songs. Much of the prophets was beyond me. The Synoptic Gospels fascinated me, but the Fourth Gospel was positively wordy. Paul was ununderstandable for the most part, and that impression stayed by me too long. I do not recall even reading Hebrews. The Revelation of St. John was my favorite book. However, the perseverance of saints is a popularly misunderstood Calvinistic dogma; I hoped that since I was persevering I might become a saint.

Having wrestled through the Bible, I was ready to give my opinion of it. It was not a book but *the* book. Why? Because I was told so. That is why I had to read it. It was chiefly about God, therefore it was holy. It was so holy that no other book was ever laid on top of it as it reposed on my bedside table. It was written in old-fashioned English and seemed to be divided into two main parts. It was a trustworthy guide for all my thinking, and it had been known to stop bullets in battle. It was quite a book; it was quite *the* book, even when it didn't make sense.

Of course, during this period I was in constant attendance at church and Sunday school. There, too, the uniqueness of the Bible was axiomatic. Mother seldom asked me what the points of the sermon were; but I had to know the "text." When the minister announced the Scripture lesson, we "turned up the place;" he waited until the congregation did so. An American congregation trusts its minister to read it correctly, without checking on him, and leaves the Bible at home. In Sunday school we memorized the Psalms (in metre) and studied the selected portions of Scripture with avidity because we were examined on them once a year. If we did well we received book prizes. That was one way of acquiring a library.

THE WORDS OF THE BIBLE

In 1924 I entered the Divinity Hall of Glasgow University. There, and later at Union Theological Seminary in New York City, I learned four facts which helped me to understand the Bible better and which gave me a more critical and a more satisfactory comprehension of it.

1. LINGUISTIC

I had been aware, somehow, that the King James Version of the Bible was an English translation of two volumes, one of which had been written in Hebrew and the other in Greek. Two professors undertook to prove that this was true by making us read chunks of Scripture in the original languages. We were not amused. But that way led to a B.D. degree, so we sweated over these unknown tongues. Our comments were numerous, but they were not meant to be blasphemous. One student remarked that he understood why Jahweh had so much trouble with the Children of Israel; He probably didn't understand them. He didn't even have Davidson's *Hebrew Grammar* to help Him. Greek was not so bad, because we had learned Greek in the Arts course. Dr. George Milligan fascinated us by showing that the New Testament was written in the common language of the ordinary man of the first century.[2] It was the *koiné,* the normal language of the average person, and not "Holy Ghost Greek," the heavenly "King's English" of the Realm of God, spoken by the Holy Spirit and those in glory, and dictated to the author or authors of the biblical books.

The results were worth the struggle. Today, in sermon preparation, I turn to the Greek, even to the Hebrew text. I wrestle with dictionaries and commentaries and "Theological Word Books" so that I may grasp what the Bible means when it uses certain expressions. Whole sermons spring out of the meaning of words, the content of phrases, the intent of ideas. It is wise to know what Isaiah had in mind by "Faith," and John by "Life," and Paul by "Love" before one talks about what these men were driving at when they used the terms. The Bible may not use "sin" and "righteousness" and "the Church" as we hope and even assert that it does.

For those of us unfortunate enough to be unable to use the original tongues there is a partial aid to the grasp of biblical meanings. We must have in front of us, on our desks at all times, for constant study, a variety of translations into English. If we can supplement these by

[2] See that valuable dictionary, J. H. Moulton and G. Milligan, *The Vocabulary of the Greek New Testament illustrated from the papyri and other non-literary sources* (London: Hodder and Stoughton, 1930).

a knowledge of the French or German or Latin versions, so much the better. By careful comparison of the renderings, aided by a perusal of the commentaries, one has a right to hope that he will grasp with some accuracy the real sense of a passage. I shall always be grateful to Moffatt for Romans XVI, and to Goodspeed for The Prayer of Manasseh. If you want to see what can be done homiletically with the English translations, read, with discrimination, the volumes by H. E. Luccock on the preaching values in the new translations. And now we have the Revised Standard Version as another, almost an "authorized," rendition to give us a more accurate rendering of the original languages.

From seven years of teaching preaching I have rediscovered what I first found in the Hebrew and Greek classrooms of the Divinity Hall of Glasgow University. One of the primary reasons that a sermon is dishonest, if not incomprehensible, is that the preacher has not made himself familiar with the meaning of a word as the writer intended it. It is an unhappy moment when one learns that Isaiah did not mean by faith what we do. It is even worse when we dig up the fact that Paul did not mean by faith what Isaiah did—"the acceptance of God's grace" and "faithfulness" may be related, but they are not identical. Linguistic studies are necessary to a competent grasp of the words of the Bible. Such comprehension is the result of sweat and tears, if not of blood.

2. LITERARY

This linguistic discovery led almost simultaneously to another. The Bible was not a book; it was not even a book in two volumes. It was a library. It contained stories and poetry and law; history and philosophy and sermons; biography and letters and prognostications. Look at the titles of the first four chapters in Julius A. Bewer's *The Literature of the Old Testament*: "Early Poems;" "Early Narratives;" "Early Laws;" "The Growth of Historical Literature." [3] That gives one an idea that the Bible is a unique book in a way that my mother never thought of when she gave me that birthday copy, and as no one had told me in church or Sunday school so that I remembered it. R. G. Moulton, in his old but classic volume, *The Literary Study of the Bible*, has placed every reader under his debt who would read the Bible with literate intelligence.[4] I do not need to stress this approach to an understanding of the Scripture; the Liberal Arts College knows its value and exposes its students to courses on the Bible as literature.

[3] New York: The Columbia University Press (revised edition, 1944). This and its companion volume, E. F. Scott, *The Literature of the New Testament* (1932), are useful sources of reference.

[4] New York: D. C. Heath and Company, 1899.

But as we excitedly work our way through the sixty-six volumes in this library, we make other discoveries. There are books within the sixty-six books which are bound as The Book. In Genesis there are the documents known as J, E and D, and R. H. Pfeiffer is now popularizing another, the S source.[5] For years it has been believed that Isaiah, like Gaul, was divided into three parts; now my students tell me that there were two Hoseas. The Synoptic Problem has had suggested as a solution that Mark and Q, and M or L are the sources used by Matthew and Luke. Paul wrote at least four letters to the troublesome saints in Corinth. It is really a tremendously exciting piece of research, and the end is not yet.

Is this important for preaching? Of course it is. One should not evaluate poetry as one does prose. One does not expect legislation to be eternal. One knows that if four biographies are written about the same person there will be differences of emphasis, even contradictions among them. The literary study of the Bible will make one pause before he treats a text as he wishes. He will be anxious, for the sake of truth, to know what the author of the passage was seeking to do with it.

When I hear students complaining about the require-

[5] *Introduction to the Old Testament* (New York: Harper and Brothers, 1941).

ments of the "core curriculum," that it spends too much time on textual problems and literary analysis, I wonder if they realize the importance of this kind of study for the message from the pulpit. How otherwise can the thoughtful member be answered who wants to know why there seems to be confusion as to how many animals were taken into the Ark; and how Isaiah, who lived in the days of Assyria's triumph, could know about Cyrus unless he lived to be over a hundred; and why there is disagreement between Matthew and John about the time of the cleansing of the Temple? The place to start answering these questions is in the seminary, in the classrooms which wrestle with the literary problems in the Old and New Testaments.

3. HISTORICAL

There is a third fact to be learned, remembered, and used from the seminary classroom. One cannot wrestle with the Bible as literature for long before one realizes that there is a great period in time between the earliest and latest writings within its covers. That is not always remembered by the preacher. Dr. Horace Taft, the founder of the Taft School, tells of a letter home from a small boy at the Pomfret School. Describing its chapel, he wrote: "The windows are beautiful. They are blue and gold and other colors and have pictures of the *men who were famous in God's time*." [6] That is a conclusion about the characters in the Bible reached by more than school boys. Once upon a time, in the days of the Bible, there was "God's time." What word describes our times is a matter of debate. But even biblically, "God's time" was quite a few years judged by man's measurement. The biblical literature was composed and edited over a span of more than twelve hundred years, from before the eleventh century B.C. until the second century A.D.

How do we come to such a judgment? History helps us to it. Biblical history sketches in broad outline, then fills in the details of some clans in the Fertile Crescent which, after a succession of migrations, settled in Palestine, in a variety of diplomatic relations with the civilizations which centered on the Nile Valley, on the Tigris and Euphrates Rivers, and in Greece and Italy. It tells of internal dissensions and of foreign policy; it sings of heroes and of the rise and fall of kings; it shows us a people's life as it was focused on altar, temple, synagogue and church. Therefore, it is essential for the student of the Bible to nail down in his memory a succession of outstanding dates, the events which occurred

[6] *Memories and Opinions* (New York: The Macmillan Company, 1942), p. 300.

then, and the books which were written around them, so that he may line up the story of Israel in a series of "before and after" the specific occasions.

Here is my own list, perhaps not as accurate as it should be, but a guide to the connection between historical happenings and biblical books:

B.C.		
c. 1250	Invasion of Palestine	Joshua
1250-1050	Settlement of Palestine	Judges
1050-931	Saul, David, and Solomon	I and II Samuel, I Kings
931	Split in Kingdom	
875-850	Ahab and Elijah	I Kings
785-745	Jeroboam II	Amos and Hosea
740-700	Expansion of Assyria	Isaiah
722	Fall of Northern Kingdom	II Kings
621	Book of the Law	Deuteronomy
612	Fall of Assyria	Nahum
612-597	Expansion of Babylonia	Jeremiah and II Kings
586	Fall of Jerusalem	
586-538	Captivity in Babylon	Ezekiel and II Isaiah

B.C.		
538-332	Overlordship of Persia	Nehemiah, Ezra, P code, Proverbs, Job
332	Alexander	
332-168	Ptolemies and Seleucids	Ecclesiastes
168-63	Maccabean Dynasty	Daniel
63	Pompey and the Beginning of Roman Rule	
A.D.		
c. 30	Ministry, Death and Resurrection of Jesus	The Gospels
30-70	The Early Church	The Acts, Paul
70	The Fall of Jerusalem	
70-150 ?	The Later New Testament Church	Pastorals, General Epistles, Revelation

That may seem a fantastic amount to keep in one's memory. In despair one recalls the subtitle of *1066 and All That*: "A Memorable History of England, Comprising, all the Parts You Can Remember, Including One Hundred and Three Good Things, Five Bad Kings, and Two Genuine Dates." [7] Yet these biblical dates are necessary pegs on which to hang the historical events and man's

[7] By W. C. Sellar and R. J. Yeatman (New York: Dutton & Company, 1931).

reactions to them as recorded in Scripture. One begins to understand an author, at least in part, by his political and cultural background.

Of course, there is much collateral reading to be done so that the background and foreground of an Amos, an Ezekiel, a Daniel, a Paul may be illuminated. I shall not easily forget the impact of Vladimir G. Simkhovitch's *Toward the Understanding of Jesus* when first I read it as a Scottish Fellow at Union Theological Seminary in 1927.[8] Here, for the first time in my life, Jesus was interpreted as one whose teachings had to be understood in the light of the Jewish-Roman struggle which led to the fall of Jerusalem in 70 A.D. I realize now that the thesis of this economic-historian is overdrawn and biased. But I also realize the truth in his method: Any biblical event is explained to some extent by its historical background and foreground. That is the stage setting against which the Biblical characters act. And the settings vary from century to century, and so do the lines in the actors' mouths. Therefore to appreciate the lines we have to grasp the influence of the settings. So we turn to the historians, secular and Jewish, cultural and economic: books like Robinson's *A History of Israel*,[9] *The Cambridge An-*

---

[8] New York: The Macmillan Company, 1927.
[9] Oxford: Clarendon Press, 1932, 2 volumes.

cient History,[10] Fleming James' *Personalities of the Old Testament*,[11] and Jackson and Lake's *The Beginnings of Christianity*,[12] monographs such as F. C. Grant's *The Economic Background of the Gospels*[13] and T. R. Glover's *The World of the New Testament*.[14] These books will help us to understand why the idea of God changes as Jerusalem's foreign policy changes and vice versa; why there was the construction of the Maginot Line of Judaism in the face of Hellenism; why Pauline universalism had to clash with the Judaisers.

It is therefore essential for preaching that we do a thorough job of preparation in the B.D. course in Old Testament and New Testament. It may be wise for seminaries to put into the "core curriculum" at least a semester's course on the Apocrypha and the Pseudepigrapha as a bridge between the Old and New Testaments. It is there that we find the genesis of such ideas as the Son of Man Messiah, the Kingdom of God, and the resurrection of the body. The minister in the parish would do well to continue his studies along such lines, so that he may have a surer grasp of the manner and

[10] New York: The Macmillan Company, 1934, particularly Volumes III, IV, VI, VII and X.

[11] New York: Charles Scribner's Sons, 1940.

[12] New York: The Macmillan Company, 1920, particularly Volumes I and V.

[13] New York: Oxford University Press, 1926.

[14] New York: Cambridge University Press, 1931.

the matter of the scriptural author he is theoretically expounding.

4. "Tendency Writing"

There is a fourth, and for the time being a last, fact to be remembered by the sermon writer about the written word. Behind the books are men and women. They have the enthusiasms, the prejudices, the partialities of men and women. These traits are inevitably incorporated in what they think and say and write. The Germans name this fact *Tendenzschrift* or *Tendenzliteratur*: writing, literature with a tendentious quality, a drift in a desired direction, a purposeful twisting of the raw material of their books. To know the truth more accurately in any given situation, such intention must be understood and may have to be discounted. Thus the D interpretation of history seeks to confine all history within the theory that goodness leads to prosperity and evil to disaster. That is obvious if we study the real preface to the book of Judges as it is found in chapters 2:6—3:6. There is summarized the cycle of human behavior which is to be illustrated graphically in the rest of the book: The Children of Israel forget God; they are defeated and oppressed by one or more of the neighboring tribes; they cry unto God in repentance; a judge (i.e. champion) is raised up; they are delivered and worship God in gratitude. Then they forget Him and the cycle begins again. That is illustrated in chapter 3:7-11:

> And the people of Israel did what was evil in the sight of the Lord, forgetting the Lord their God, and serving the Baals and the Asheroth. Therefore the anger of the Lord was kindled against Israel, and he sold them into the hand of Cushanrishathaim king of Mesopotamia; and the people of Israel served Cushanrishathaim eight years. But when the people of Israel cried to the Lord, the Lord raised up a deliverer for the people of Israel, who delivered them, Othniel the son of Kenaz, Caleb's younger brother. The Spirit of the Lord came upon him, and he judged Israel; he went out to war, and the Lord gave Cushanrishathaim king of Mesopotamia into his hand; and his hand prevailed over Cushanrishathaim. So the land had rest forty years. Then Othniel the son of Kenaz died.

Verse 12 reads:

> And the people of Israel again did what was evil in the sight of the Lord; and the Lord strengthened Eglon the king of Moab against Israel, because they had done what was evil in the sight of the Lord.

The P interpretation argues for a theocracy mediated through a hierocracy. Thus in the P document Noah makes no sacrifice to God after his deliverance from the flood. How could he? He was a layman. As worthy a man as Noah would never have usurped priestly functions. But in the J document, which had no such scruples, Noah built an altar and "took of every clean beast and of every clean fowl" and made so successful a burnt offering that the Lord, smelling the "sweet savour" vowed never to overwhelm the earth again. When Noah brought the animals into the Ark, according to the J document, he took clean animals and birds "by sevens, the male and the female" (Genesis 7:2) so as to have enough both to sacrifice and to replenish the earth.

In like manner, Jonah is discovered to be the villain of a spiritual tract which pleads for the universality of God against a too narrow particularism. The Pauline loss of temper in Galatians has to be felt in the strained atmosphere of well-meaning Judaisers. Paul is so determined that his position is the only valid Christian one that he not only "withstood him (Peter) to face," but he passed such a judgment on those who unsettled the Galatians that the King James Version would not literally translate the ejaculation into English (5:12). Nahum should be read along with the last chapters of II Kings, and Ruth as a reaction to Ezra. The suggestion that Acts was prepared for Paul's defense before Caesar may be a clue to the pro-Roman bias of the book. Why is it that time after time in Acts the Romans are whitewashed and the Jews are blackwashed? (E.g. 2:23; 3:13,

7:51-53; 10:1-48; 16:35-40; 18:12-17; 19:28-40; 22:22-29; 23:16-35; 24:22-23; 26:30-32.)

To understand this tendency-writing, we shall have to be familiar with the linguistic, literary and historical approaches to Scripture. Then we are able to understand the messages of the books in the light of their surroundings. We shall comprehend why scholars feel that there are three Isaiahs rather than one, and why Mark is basic for Matthew and Luke. We shall sympathize with the bitter gloating of Nahum when we know how Assyria was fearfully hated in Jerusalem. We shall appreciate the overemphasis on certain aspects of the faith in the Pauline letters when we apprehend that they are "occasional" writings dealing with specific problems. We shall acknowledge the wisdom of those who question the Pauline authorship of the Pastorals because of the developed organization of the Church revealed in these three epistles. Our sermons will know what to discount as transient and what to emphasize as permanent, with a greater degree of accuracy, when we remember that the biblical writers may have been as biased as we are, and with as much honorable intention. Many of our readers have heard about this in college courses in religion; we are using the Bible they studied. They would like to think that we studied it, too, with intelligence, sympathy, and integrity. And the way to begin to do it is by serious attention to these four approaches to an intelligent understanding of the words of the Bible.

* * * * * *

We have come a long way from a mother's comment as she gave her elder son a Bible on his fifteenth birthday. He read it as instructed because it was his mother's desire and because, to some extent, he appreciated it as *the* book. But it took the courses in the Divinity School and continued study thereafter to make him understand it as he does now.

May I therefore make an appeal to seminary students and those in the pastorate to pore over the Bible and the collateral reading, so that there may be brought to the folk in the pew a reasoned and reasonable understanding of the volume in which our faith is revealed. We have not yet discovered what the revelation is, but we have sought to understand the mode of its revealing. *A priori,* it is not unlikely that the form will have an effect on the matter itself.

Professor James Stalker of Glasgow had a high conception of the ministry. In giving the "charge" to the minister at an induction service he once said:

> I like to think of the minister as only one of the congregation set apart by the rest for a particular purpose. They

say to him: Look, brother, we are busy with our daily toils, and confused with cares, but we eagerly long for peace and light to illuminate our life, and we have heard there is a land where these are to be found, a land of repose and joy, full of thoughts that breathe and words that burn, but we cannot go thither ourselves. We are too embroiled in daily cares. Come, we will elect you, and set you free from toil, and you shall go thither for us and week by week trade with that land and bring us its treasures and its spoils.[15]

What its treasures and its spoils are we shall consider in the next chapter, but how are we to bring them back to our people if we do not know where to explore and with what to search? We have at our disposal the tools for the investigation, if we will but learn how to make use of them.

[15] Alexander Gammie, *Preachers I Have Heard* (Glasgow: Pickering and Inglis, c. 1946), pp. 44-45.

II

The Word of God

WE have been talking about the Bible, about how to read it with intelligence so that we may learn what it is all about. We have found that it is a library of books, comprising various types of literature, written in Hebrew or Greek over a period of twelve hundred years, revealing the personal predilections and idiosyncrasies of the authors. Is that what the Bible is? Yes. The findings are, I believe, basically true, though there may be minor errors in the dating or in the interpretation. But the question pops up again with an addendum: "Is that really what the Bible is? Hasn't something been left out?" We must admit that there is an omission. Our answers are not wrong, but they are incomplete. What has been left out? It is the something which my mother believed was there when she wrote on the flyleaf, "Commit thy way unto the Lord; trust also in him; and he shall bring it to pass." The Bible is about God; it has to do with God. God is in it, all through it, all over it. He meets you on every page. He cannot be avoided in Scripture. If, like the Psalmist, we asked the question:

> Whither shall I go from thy spirit?
> Or whither shall I flee from thy presence?
> (PSALM 139:7)

the answer might well be: "Don't try the Bible." It is God, or something about God, that gives to this library, written in so many styles at such diverse times, its unity, that allows it to be bound as one book. In Him the Bible coheres. Therefore, while we have not been wrong in analyzing it from four aspects, our study has not been completed. We must now try to locate and explicate the synthesizing factor.

Perhaps there is a clue in the phrase "The Canon of Scripture." "Canon" meant originally a reed, then a measuring line or rule. When applied to the Bible, it denotes that normative collection or list of books which is accepted by a church as inspired Holy Scripture. The touchstone is divine inspiration; the books accepted are regarded as containing the word of God. But what in Scripture is to be regarded as "the word of God"? That is a matter for a series of articles in itself; but let me jump quickly to what is—for me—the heart of the matter. As I study the Bible, one fact continually asks to be considered seriously, namely, that God is constantly seeking to bring man into such relations with Himself that He and man may be on friendly terms and that man may be spiritually healthy. That is—for me—the central meaning of the deliverance from Egypt, of the idea of a Covenant relationship, of the raising of the Judges, of the preaching of the Prophets, of the return of the remnant from Exile, of the cultus of the Law, of the Incarnation of our Lord, of the presence of the Holy Spirit and of the establishment of the Church. The word of God is not primarily the words of the Bible. It is not essentially accurate to talk of the Bible as the word of God. The word of God is the activity of God, in constantly seeking to bring man into such relations with Himself that man understands that this is what gives sense to his life on earth. Despite man's misunderstanding of God's desire, despite his refusal of God's offer of friendship, despite his seeking the meaning of life in himself, God keeps coming back with yet another offer of good understanding. God does not do this because man deserves it, or works for it, but because that is the kind of God He is—a God of love, of good will to man. That activity of God, seen in so many events in the pages of the Old and New Testaments, is what is meant by "Salvation" and "Justification" and "Adoption" and "Redemption" and the like. That is the "Good

News" of the Bible from beginning to end. It is the Gospel found in Exodus as in Matthew, preached by Second Isaiah and by St. Paul, broadcast by the Book of the Law in 621 B.C. and incarnated in Jesus at the beginning of the Christian era. The God, who is the same yesterday, today and forever, never had any other purpose for man from the Creation until now. Therefore, thanks be to God for His unspeakable gift, which He was always giving, and which was uniquely revealed in Jesus Christ our Lord. The Incarnation is but the Biblical climax of a repeated revelation. Therefore, when we speak of the "Word of God" with a capital W, we mean not only its becoming flesh in Jesus of Nazareth, but also that divine, creative succession of attempts by God to prove to man that He was a God who cared for him, and who would not rest until man found his peace and his joy in a willing acceptance of the relationship with Him. This relationship God, because of His character and will, was compelled to offer in order to be, and to continue to be, God.

Here is how a group of Duke students and their teacher put that fact after much debate and with numerous emendations:

God, the Creator and Sustainer of life, has so purposed in His love that man be in right relations with Him, that of

His own free will He overcomes the power and erases the guilt of sin which separates man from God. This was always His effective purpose, but it was uniquely manifested and dramatized in the birth, life, death and resurrection of Jesus. He is acknowledged as the Son of God because he supremely reveals the will and nature of God. This redeeming activity of God is perpetuated by the working of the Holy Spirit. Those who believe this are bound in an eternal fellowship whose daily life on earth is marked by faith, love and hope. Those who refuse to believe this are under the judgment of God's love, here and hereafter.

That attempt to state the Word of God is not perfect. We have enough of a sense of humor, if not of humility, to refuse to believe that creation has been groaning and travailing for hundreds of years to produce a professor and a class which would say the definitive word on the Word of God. But we believe we are not entirely wrong. Why were we not content to use the Apostles' Creed? It was not because of the reason usually offered: that the Creed ignores the earthly life of our Lord. Dr. Powell Davies once objected whimsically to it on that ground, when he remarked: "Jesus' ministry is designated only by the comma placed between 'born of the Virgin Mary,' and 'suffered under Pontius Pilate' "! Our criticism was that it ignored the Old Testament, except for the phrase "Maker of heaven and earth." The whole

Bible reveals the Word of God, which was, and is, and will continue to be.

*　*　*　*　*　*

Now, notice what this means for our use of the Bible in preaching.

In the first place, it means that we have but one theme to preach on: the fact that God sought and seeks men so that they may be in right relations with Him and with one another. When they are in such relations, they are "righteous." That is the biblical *Weltanschauung*, its World-view. I wish there were a better word than *Weltanschauung*, but thus far it has not turned up— maybe "World-view" is an adequate translation. "Gospel" and "Evangel" are already too limited; most of us think of them as New Testament terms. This World-view is the burden of our sermons. We have no right to claim the sanction of Holy Writ for any text which does not deal with some aspect of this World-view. Moreover, the Word of God is not limited to the pages of the Bible. That redeeming activity of God is today perpetuated by the work of His Holy Spirit in the believer, who is in the community of believers, which is the Church. That is why every sermon must be an "expository" sermon. Our job as preachers is to expound the World-view, in the confident belief that the active Word of God may again bring to pass an act of reconciliation, of salvation.

In the second place, it means that we have the Old Testament as a source of the World-view, as well as the New. That is not heresy. It has been orthodoxy since the Church rebelled against Marcion in the second century. Counter to his Canon of Scriptures, which rejected much of the Old Testament, the Church was forced to define its Canon, and so began the process of spelling out the acceptable writings, which more or less came to completion in 367 A.D. under Athanasius. There has been controversy since then about the inclusion of the Apocrypha; that is outside our immediate purpose. What is important for us to realize is that the Old Testament canon as well as the New Testament canon together make up our Biblical canon. This is not just Presbyterian doctrine. Here is Article VII of the Thirty-nine Articles of Religion: "The Old Testament is not contrary to the New: for both in the Old and New Testament everlasting life is offered to Mankind by Christ. . . ." The Old Testament is not merely a forerunner for the New; God's purpose was effective there also. Where can you find a more beautiful expression of Justification by Faith than in the Call of Isaiah? Listen to it:

> In the year that King Uzziah died I saw the Lord sitting upon a throne, high and lifted up; and his train filled the temple. Above him stood the seraphim; each had six wings:

with two he covered his face, and with two he covered his
feet, and with two he flew. And one called to another and
said:

> "Holy, holy, holy is the Lord of hosts;
> the whole earth is full of his glory."

And the foundations of the thresholds shook at the voice
of him who called, and the house was filled with smoke.
And I said: "Woe is me! For I am lost; for I am a man of
unclean lips, and I dwell in the midst of a people of unclean lips; for my eyes have seen the King, the Lord of
Hosts!"

Then flew one of the seraphim to me, having in his hand
a burning coal which he had taken with tongs from the altar.
And he touched my mouth, and said: "Behold, this has
touched your lips; your guilt is taken away, and your sin
forgiven." And I heard the voice of the Lord saying, "Whom
shall I send, and who will go for us?" Then I said, "Here
I am! Send me."

(ISAIAH 6:1-8)

What did he do to have his sins forgiven? Nothing. What
works justified him? None. One of God's ministers
touched his lips and said, "thine iniquity is taken away,
and thy sin purged." That is God's grace in action, accepted by man.

When Paul sought the man of faith, whom did he
choose? Peter? Himself? No, Abraham.

Thus Abraham "believed God, and it was reckoned to him as righteousness." So you see that it is men of faith who are the sons of Abraham. And the Scripture, foreseeing that God would justify the Gentiles by faith, preached the gospel beforehand to Abraham saying, "In thee shall all the nations be blessed." So then, those who are men of faith are blessed with Abraham who had faith.

(GALATIANS 3:6-9)

You can't go much further back in the Old Testament than that without sliding off the edge. This is not to deny the place of our Lord Jesus Christ; there God's Word is incarnate as never before. But it is to plead for the whole Bible in the pulpit. Too many of us are pragmatic Marcionites in our use of Scripture.

In the third place, it means that the eternal Word of God is always cabined, cribbed and confined by the temporal and material facts in which it reveals itself. The temporal conditions the eternal; it conceals the Word as well as revealing it; it mumbles or stammers or mispronounces the Word. And the result is misunderstanding and hence heresy.

This need not surprise us. Even the orthodox theory of the Incarnation makes our Lord perfectly man as well as perfectly God. He is not "Man" with a capital M; there is no such abstraction for Christian faith. He is not even The Jew, with a capital T. He was the Word of

God become the flesh of a Galilean Jew of the first century A.D., who belonged to the people of the land, at a time when Palestine was a Roman dependency, policed by an army of occupation. Now many people don't like that. In fact, they refuse to believe it. One of my students wrote a Ku Klux Klan leader, who had been in favor of anti-Semitic action, asking him if he did not believe that Jesus was a Jew. The answer was brief: "No. He was the Son of God." Yet the Son of God spoke Aramaic; he earned his living as a carpenter in Nazareth; he worshipped in the Synagogue and Temple; he was educated by the Pharisees; he was true to the Word of God as it had been transmitted by his race. That is why we must use the linguistic, literary, historical, and tendency-writing approaches to understand him. That is why Torrey sought to render the Gospels into Aramaic and then into English so that we might catch the Galilean accent and the nuances of Jesus' speech.[1] That is why Simkhovitch and Grant studied the historical and economic background.[2] That is why there will always be room for more and new lives of Jesus which seek to see him acting on the stage of his own time and place.

If that is true of the study of Jesus, then realize how

[1] C. H. Torrey, *The Four Gospels* (New York: Harper and Brothers, 1933).

[2] See above, pp. 14, 15.

it is also true of the Old Testament revelations of the Word of God. What is the value of the Covenant conception? What is at the heart of the idea of sacrifice? What is implied by the concept of a Remnant? What is the common ground on which prophet and priest stand? What is the import of the messianic hope? We must carefully strip away that which is incidental and transient so as to find the basic pronouncement as it is related to the Word of God. The eternal significance of the Word is wrapped around with the error and the littleness and the sin of its hearers and receivers and interpreters. It is because of this that so many Protestants of all denominations refuse to equate the Word of God with the Bible, or to see the Word among men only in Jesus of Nazareth. Roland Bainton of Yale states the position of Martin Luther in these words:

> The Bible for him was not strictly identical with the Word of God. God's Word is the work of redemption in Christ which became concrete in Scripture as God in Christ became incarnate in the flesh; and as Christ by the incarnation was not denuded of human characteristics, so the Scripture as the medium of the Word was not divested of human limitations.[3]

Our response is "Amen."

[3] *Here I Stand* (Nashville: Abingdon-Cokesbury Press, 1950), p. 331.

So, then, we have but one theme to preach on: the World-view of the Bible, the Word of God in action, found in the Old Testament and the New, and to be dug out of its human environment by the methods we discussed in the previous chapter. John Knox sums up, in a single sentence, our job as we begin to wrestle with the meaning of a section of Scripture: "The event is the important thing, not the account; and we must *interpret* the account to recover the event." [4]

* * * * * *

A practical question arises now: How can we preach this World-view? In what way shall we use the Bible in showing our congregations this idea of a God who is constantly seeking them in love? Here are three suggestions.

One method is to take the key words which seek in small compass to embrace the theological World-view of the Bible. Why are so many Presbyterian churches named "Covenant"? What is the root idea in the agreement God made with the children of Israel under Moses? Wherein does a "covenant" God differ from a local deity? What does that mean for the human partner to the compact? What did Jeremiah mean when he talked

[4] *Criticism and Faith* (Nashville: Abingdon-Cokesbury Press, 1952), p. 80.

about the new covenant which would involve the law written in the heart (31:31-34)? Is the idea of the covenant still of value to help us to understand God's act and man's response? Did the Scottish Covenanters have this idea in mind? Does the Church of the Covenant in your home town live up to its name?

Some of you know an Episcopal Church which is named "Grace." What is grace? Why is it so important for Paul? Is it as important for us as it was for the Apostle to the Gentiles? Should it be? Should folk be allowed to become members of Grace Church who do not believe the strong, winsome, encouraging theological idea which the name of their parish commemorates?

Another way to preach the good news of the Word of God is to seek to expound the significance of a biblical event: that is, a fact in history with its meaningful interpretation. The God of the Bible is a God who acts in history; the Bible is the account of the remembered meaning which one generation passed on to another as too significant to be forgotten.[5] History, then, is event plus interpretation. God acts and man responds—sometimes for his own good, sometimes disastrously—and the encounter is construed for others to understand. Why is the Passover observed annually by the Jew? What does

[5] See C. H. Dodd, *The Bible Today* (New York: The Macmillan Company, 1947), chapter V.

he recall then about God and man encountering each other? What does the memory do to him and for him? Remember that the men of the Bible were not abstract thinkers who wrestled with concepts, but people who watched for signs of God's activity in the world of events and spelled out particular happenings as revelations of God's character and will. From the Passover it is but a step to the Resurrection, that central fact in the New Testament, which is of even greater importance theologically than the Crucifixion.

Have you read Nahum recently, that fiery nationalist who gloated over the ruin of Nineveh in exciting and gripping verse? Listen to him:

> Woe to the bloody city,
> all full of lies and booty—
> no end to the plunder!
> The crack of whip, and rumble of wheel,
> galloping horse and bounding chariot!
> Horsemen charging,
> flashing sword and glittering spear,
> hosts of slain,
> heaps of corpses,
> dead bodies without end—
> they stumble over the bodies!
> And all for the countless harlotries
>   of the harlot,
> graceful and of deadly charms,

who betrays nations with her harlotries,
and people with her charms.

Behold I am against you,
says the Lord of hosts,
and will lift up your skirts over your face;
and I will let nations look on your nakedness
and kingdoms on your shame.
I will throw filth at you
and treat you with contempt,
and make you a gazingstock.
And all who look on you will shrink from
  you and say,
Wasted is Nineveh; who will bemoan her?
Whence shall I seek comforters for her?
                    (NAHUM 3:1-7)

What can we learn from this jingoist of Judah who out-
Kiplings Kipling? Isn't he wrong in his whole outlook?
No. He is right in believing in a God who acts in history.
But he is wrong in limiting God's action to intervention
on behalf of a chosen people. The author of Jonah knew
something about God's attitude to Nineveh that Nahum
never grasped. Nahum is a good example of a book
whose truth is encased in error, where the eternal Word
is almost shouted down by the voice of the man who
expounds it.

A third way to preach the Word of God is biographically. This is understandable, even inevitable. As the Word had to become flesh and dwell among us in Jesus of Nazareth in order that we could the more easily understand God, so His Word is made clearer for our hearers to grasp when it becomes flesh in biblical characters. Jacob, that shrewd rascal with a sensitivity for religion, is not far removed from many of our communicants. We, too, know—maybe we are—Jonahs who prefer to serve God in our way rather than His, and who have to be re-educated. Thomas, that disciple from the Missouri section of Galilee, can become a missionary only when he experiences the resurrected Christ.

There are three ways to preach the Word of God as it is revealed in the Bible. Such an understanding of it will keep us from the hysteria of burning or banning those sections of the translations which do not agree with our previously conceived ideas, or from the more common practice of ignoring them. It will also keep us from the plague of the small text, the two or three words plucked from Scripture into which we read our own interpretation. As long ago as 1870 John A. Broadus, in his classic textbook on preaching, warned of the danger of eisegesis. And he was a Southern Baptist! [6]

There, then, are three suggestions for handling the

[6] *On the Preparation and Delivery of Sermons* (New York: Harper and Brothers, copyright, 1870; revised 1944), pp. 36-43.

THE TRUE AND LIVELY WORD

World-view of the Bible—by key words, by historical interpretation and by biographical sketches.

* * * * * *

The study of the Bible has passed through two phases into a third for us. The first was that of "Infallibility." It was an easy age to preach in. When one had a command of sufficient "proof" texts, he could quote the apposite one and so end any argument. A shrewdly chosen scriptural quotation, used with a thump on the pulpit Bible, meant Q.E.D. for the minister's side of the argument. That is implied in the Scottish beadle's reply to the question: "Is your minister a good preacher?" "Guid? Man, he has dinged the guts oot o' three pu'pit Bibles." [7] There are some, maybe many, who preach as if these days were still with us.

The second phase was one of "Dissection." Under the impetus of the lower and higher criticism the Bible seemed to be torn to shreds. Moses did not write the Pentateuch, and John was not the author of the Fourth Gospel. There is more than one story of creation and several contradictory accounts of the Resurrection. David did not compose all the Psalms nor Paul all the letters ascribed to him. It was an age in which students in

[7] The beadle is the Scottish equivalent of the verger or sexton.

theology seemed to revel in the spiritual chaos they were creating. It was asserted that if a thesis could have proved that Jesus was a woman, the University of Tübingen would have awarded the candidate a Ph.D. degree *summa cum laude*. It is not to be wondered at that Modernism was hated and biblical criticism shunned by the average Fundamentalist.

But a third era is with us, a good one. It knows that there is truth in both positions and seeks to capture each within a new synthesis. It realizes that the Fundamentalist was right in appreciating the fact of a God who moved into history in a saving way, as recounted in the Bible. The Bible is still the source book of a World-view that is eternally valid. It also realizes that the Modernist was right in insisting that the Bible could be understood best only with the help of linguistic, literary and historical analysis, which revealed the bent and bias of the writers' minds. Therefore this new phase, which is to be designated neither as one of "Infallibility" nor of "Dissection" but of "Appreciation," seeks to understand the Bible as the experiences of a religious community which over hundreds of years sought to explain and define the way of God with men. That is the thesis of John Knox' little volume on *Criticism and Faith*, which succeeds in showing the value of biblical criticism for preaching, especially in the New Testament. That is why the authors of *Biblical Authority for Today* have included in their symposium five pages on "Guiding Principles for the Interpretation of the Bible, as accepted by the Ecumenical Study Conference at Wadham College, Oxford, 1949." [8] Here is an abbreviated synopsis of the four points made there: First, any teaching that clearly contradicts the biblical position cannot be accepted as Christian. Second, one must start with an historical and critical examination of the passage. Third, the biblical teaching on social and political issues must be viewed in the light of the tension between life in the kingdoms of this world and participation in the Kingdom of God. Fourth, the Bible speaks primarily to the Church . . . (and) leads us back to the living Word of God.

It is only by such criticism, applied with trenchancy and reverence, that we may discern what the Word of God was to its interpreters and therefore may be for us. If God is truth rather than tradition, as Tertullian—I think—once remarked, then we must handle the word of

[8] Edited by Alan Richardson and Wolfgang Schweitzer (Philadelphia: The Westminster Press, 1952). See pp. 240-244. One of my colleagues at Duke Divinity School, Dr. Kenneth W. Clark, completed a chapter at Christmas, 1952, for a *Festschrift* in honor of Johannes de Zwann, Professor of New Testament at the University of Leyden. His paper was entitled "Textual Criticism and Doctrine." His closing paragraph is: "Therefore, it is the great responsibility of textual criticism to refine the New Testament text toward an ever increasing purity. It must lay the foundation on which alone doctrinal interpretation of the New Testament may be soundly based."

truth rightly, and rightly means with accuracy and care as well as with devotion. We are fortunate enough to live in a period when *The Interpreter's Bible* is being published, which is a symbol of the era of "Appreciation." [9] Here are combined exegesis and exposition, neither of which by itself can give us the World-view; together they may, if we use the commentary with honesty.

* * * * * *

Let me conclude this chapter with a personal confession. I am not one who has been able thus far to make much use of so-called books of devotion, classical or modern. I have found my devotional life nourished best by commentaries. For you who will not believe this, I ask you to read either Nygren on Romans [10] or Dodd on the Johannine Epistles.[11] That is why I cannot agree with, though I seek to understand, students who make too great a differentiation between the classroom and the chapel, the rostrum and the pulpit, the bench and the pew while they are in divinity school and even afterwards. One

[9] In process of publication by the Abingdon-Cokesbury Press, in 12 volumes.

[10] Anders Nygren, *Commentary on Romans* (Philadelphia: Muhlenberg Press, 1949).

[11] C. H. Dodd, *The Johannine Epistles* (New York: Harper and Brothers, 1946).

may worship in the classroom and learn in the chapel. My own experience may be summed up in a reverent alteration of a passage of Brother Lawrence's *The Practice of the Presence of God*:

> The time of research does not with me differ from the time of prayer, and in the commentaries and dictionaries of my study, . . . I possess God in as great tranquility as if I were upon my knees at the blessed sacrament.

III

The Word of the World

IT has been wisely said that though confession is good for the soul, it is bad for the reputation. Even so, I have a confession. I might as well proffer it, because you will find out the truth as you read. This third chapter has been the most difficult to write, primarily because I know even less about its subject matter than I think I do of the others. When I asked myself "What is 'The Word of the World'?", I was not so much at a loss for answers as deafened and bewildered by the variety and volume of the responses. The problem was to choose the answer which seemed to be both valid in content and pertinent to our human situation. Let me share with you, by way of introduction and definition, the association of ideas which finally answered the question for me, and I hope for you. Each one of you will be able to see understatements and overemphases in it; but I hope the main lines of the interpretation are true for all of us.

I turned to Webster to prime my thinking. One definition of the World is that it is "the sum of human affairs and interests." Immediately I had to confess that I do not know the World as defined. A verse from the Psalms popped into my mind:

> Such knowledge is too wonderful for me;
> it is high, I cannot attain it.
>
> (PSALM 139:6)

That is an illegitimate use of Scripture, but it describes my reaction to the definition. I do not know "the sum of human affairs and interests."

Perhaps an autobiographical sketch will reveal the limitations of my knowledge of the World. I was born, reared and formally educated in Glasgow. I studied the history and culture of Scotland and, to a much lesser degree, England. Then I was exposed to Rome, Greece and Palestine. The Jewish-Hellenistic strain in Western civilization so dominated my studies that, after high school, I never touched mathematics, European history or the physical sciences. On the side, I did take all the work offered at the University in political science and political philosophy. Think of the gaps there!

Although I came to study at the Union Theological Seminary in New York, I had never heard of the United States of America in the classroom. There was nary a hint as to the Revolution or the Civil War in the formal instruction I received. The Orient, too, was literally a closed book. A recent reading of F. S. C. Northrop's *The Meeting of East and West* [1] made me understand John Keats' excitement over Chapman's *Homer*:

> Then felt I like a watcher of the skies
> When a new planet swims into his ken.

I looked at myself "with a wild surmise." Was I expected to know all this, too?

Even my knowledge of "the sum of human affairs and interests" in America is limited. It excludes South America, Central America and Canada. So far as the United States is concerned it is confined, in residence, to New York City; Amherst, Massachusetts; Wallingford, Connecticut; and Durham, North Carolina. I am a Scot, with some Yankee conditioning, endeavoring to live among Southerners near the Eastern Seaboard. I may not be provincial; but I am, more or less, an alien regionalist. Should I then speak on the American Worldview when the West is known only from one fleeting

[1] New York: The Macmillan Company, 1946.

visit and the central states are a great X, a vast unknown quantity? Cleveland, Cincinnati, Dallas, Los Angeles, Tulsa I have known "by the hearing of the ear," but even their voices have been but "the breath of a light whisper." The more I reflect on my unenlightenment the more sympathy I have with the Congress, which seeks to govern a spacious continent as if it were a compact nation. Add to size the racial differences within the boundaries. Apart altogether from the white-colored problem, think of the intermingling of immigrants who, to an amazing degree, live their lives with a double loyalty, one here and one "back home." We are in a melting pot that has still not melted the various ingredients. Religiously and culturally, to change the metaphor, we are a coat of many colors.

"The Word of the World"—do I dare speak even of the Word of the "American" World?

So I tried a new tack. I recalled a definition of the World from the recesses of my memory: "The World is society as it is organized apart from God." Let us see if this helps us. The man of the World is, according to this view, set over against the Christian, for whom society should be organized in terms of God. That set my mental aberrations off in another direction, until I stumbled over a very simple question: "Is this the man you expect to preach to—the man who consciously and

willingly lives in a society organized apart from God?"
I wanted to say "Yes," but it isn't true, at least not for
this book. The average listener in the ordinary pew of
the accepted denominations is not such a man of such
a World. Yet there have been sermons vigorously addressed to the man of the World who was not present.
In the early days of his ministry, Thomas Chalmers
of Scotland divided his time between reproaching his
parishioners and lambasting Napoleon. Regarding this
division of sermonic labor, Frank W. Boreham wrote:

> Now and again, the brilliant and eloquent young
> preacher turned aside from this line of things to denounce
> the designs of Napoleon. But as the Fifeshire farmers saw
> no way in which the arguments of their minister were likely
> to come under the notice of the tyrant and turn him from
> his fell purpose of invading Britain, they were as much
> perplexed by these sermons as by the others.[2]

The young Chalmers has had successors in our century,
in sermons addressed to the Kaiser and Hitler and
Stalin. But even if we avoid this form of inanity, we
practice another. We too often scold those who are present because our attention is fixed on those who are absent.

[2] *A Bunch of Everlastings* (New York: Methodist Book Concern, 1920),
p. 9.

Some months ago I was invited to preach a "revival series" in a church in Tennessee. I wrote the minister and asked if he meant "revival" in the old-fashioned, evangelical sense, or with the dictionary denotation of "reanimation from a state of spiritual languor and depression." Were the meetings to be held in his church, or in poolrooms, saloons (if any) and secular auditoriums? Did he have in mind something like the "commando raids" of the British churches, or were these services for the deepening of the spiritual life of the parish members? He wanted the latter, in accordance with the denotation rather than the connotation of "revival." It was to be a mission for his own folk in their own kirk; if others dropped in, so much the better. The location of the service is important in deciding the type of homiletical appeal. I am beginning to see the wisdom of Billy Graham in holding his type of "revival" in a secular auditorium rather than in an ecclesiastical edifice. But we, who look forward to the generally accepted type of pulpit ministry, do not address people who consciously and willingly believe in society as organized apart from God.

So I began to come nearer the meaning of "The Word of the World" for our immediate purposes. I was thinking of the people who work in the World and worship in the Church. By the World, I mean society as it is

constructed without particular attention to the Church:
the interlocking conglomeration of the professions, busi-
nesses and trades; of the stock exchanges, the associations
of manufacturers and the trade unions; of nominal Christians and Jews and unbelievers. The folk to whom we
preach are a Jekyll-Hyde composite: the men of the
World in the Church, the men of the Church in the
World, the men of the World and of the Church, the
men in the World and in the Church. That came out in
class one day as we were analyzing the "Patterns" which
form the structure of a sermon. We were working on the
Classification (or Label) Pattern, and by way of illus-
tration we outlined on the board a sermon on the topic:
"What Kind of Christianity is Yours?". We made three
divisions. The first was Cultural Christianity, the kind
of thing we mean when we say that the United States
and Great Britain are Christian countries. If we were
to picture it as a building it would probably be a Gothic
structure, over whose door is written "Blessed is the
nation whose God is the Lord" (Psalm 33:12). That
is both definite enough and vague enough to be accepted.
The second was Churchly Christianity, the point of view
of the larger denominations. Pictorially it would be
something like the Parthenon, probably with a Corin-
thian capital and an Ionic base for its limestone pillars.
Its text would be "Come unto me, all ye that labor and

are heavy laden" (Matthew 11:28). If all come, there will have to be some compromising inside if there is to be peace. The third was Sectarian Christianity, the point of view of the little Bethels and City Missions. It would be pictured as a plain, nondescript kind of building with a small door. Its motto would be "Strait is the gate, and narrow is the way, which leadeth unto life" (Matthew 7:14). There would not be room for all that over the door, so it would be painted round the walls for the few who find it to see as they worship.

For our purposes today we are thinking primarily of the "Churchly" Christian, though members of the other classifications will worship with us. The man of the World to whom we shall preach is one who is not content with the World as his only dwelling place, but actually becomes a member of the Church for a variety of reasons. It is more than custom, or the cultural environment, or the desire for a stage for weddings and funerals, though these enter into his choice. Maybe if we examine the Word of the World which he hears and listens to and even obeys, we shall be better able to understand how to preach to him. We know that we cannot define that Word accurately or universally or finally; but we can know something of its accent and its inflections from listening to our members, especially in their non-ecclesiastical moments. These moments are not unknown in church meetings, official and unofficial.

What then is the Word of this segment of the American World with which we are acquainted, as it is heard in the Church? It is not clear enough in my own mind to be outlined in the form of a creed, as yet, but it has three significant aspects of which we should be aware before we start preaching.

1. PRAGMATIC ASSURANCE

It is a Word from a World that is remarkably sure of itself. To put it crudely but emphatically, this country is booming. Frederick Lewis Allen speaks for this point of view in the last sentences of his latest book:

> The story of the changes in the contours of American life that we have hammered out in the first half of this twentieth century, is a triumph story, however harsh may have been some of our experiences in the interim and however obscure may be the shape of the future. We do well to think of our accomplishments thus far as but the preface to what we may accomplish in the second half of the century if we can continue to invent, improve and change—and can keep a good heart. The courageous nation, like the courageous man, is not unhappy at the thought of dangers beside the road ahead, but welcomes them as challenges to be faced and overwhelmed along an adventurous course.[3]

[3] *The Big Change* (New York: Harper and Brothers, 1952), p. 293.

That was brought home to me on a motor trip to California in 1950. At point after point on the journey I was repeatedly staggered by the achievements of American man. What would be hailed as wonders of the world in Europe were almost taken for granted by the American traveller as necessary jobs done for the sake of his convenience: the four-lane boulevard across the top of the Hoover Dam; gasoline pumps six thousand feet up on the Sierra Nevada in the Sequoia National Park; the long bridges at San Francisco; the tunnel through the hills behind Berkeley. They were almost as breath-taking as the natural wonders that lie between the Atlantic and the Pacific. This fantastic technical skill of the American engineer and the overwhelming glory of nature may reach an eternal union and a temporary climax if a road is built down, across and up the Grand Canyon. The American can evidently do anything he has a mind to do; if it is impossible, it just takes longer. This proven confidence in his mechanical conquest of his world is what impresses other nations. The American soldier was gladly welcomed as a first-class fighting man; but he was matched in this regard by the soldiers of more than one allied nation. But what the Londoner will never forget was the sight of an American bulldozer of unbelievable proportions cleaning up a blitzed street the morning after a raid, with a nineteen-year-old driver skillfully maneuvering his mechanical hippopotamus one-handed, a cigarette nonchalantly dangling from his lower lip. That is symbolic of the pragmatic assurance of this country in a thousand different endeavors. The saga of America is a success story that is reckoned in monetary wealth which requires mechanical computators to figure and which has become the yardstick for estimating the good life. "The almighty dollar" is hardly the way to describe the norm. What foreigners cannot comprehend is the quantity of almighty dollars, sufficient for almost everyone to have a share, the like of which no other nation has ever known. No wonder that, when one faces this success story, he can find no competent words to describe it, but is reduced to such repetitive muttering as "Boy! Oh boy! Oh boy!"

All this has been done without much, if any, awareness of God. That is the terrifying thought that slides into one's consciousness as he ponders this superb accomplishment. It has not been done in defiance of God—just without Him. We have heard much of the secularization of our life, but here we seem to have "Exhibit A." God is not despised or obliterated; His Word has just become unnecessary. Even where He once played a part He is being ignored—not even benched, just ignored. That is true in colleges founded for religious purposes and in hospitals which originally were the expression of Christian love. This side-tracking of God is also true of British life. H. H. Farmer a decade ago wrote these words:

> Today people, even people in the churches themselves, think of religion, not as that which is relevant to, and informs, all activities, but as just one activity among others for those who happen to be inclined that way, like folk-dancing. It is something apart. The whole business of religion begins and ends in a situation of abstraction from the things that actually fill men's lives.[4]

What is the reason for this? I suppose the answer is due in part to Darwin and Marx and Freud, the most influential thinkers of the nineteenth century, and to their scientific and economic descendants. The "scientific approach" which has dominated the liberal arts colleges throughout this century has not made it easy for a religion of revelation to keep its respectability, far less its influential position. Even where there is a religious sensitivity left, it is found in such a prayer as "Lead us into the truth, come whence it may, cost what it will." That may be a good prayer, but it is hardly the petition of Christian orthodoxy, which believes that the truth has been disclosed in the Word of God. Perhaps the religion of the scientific approach

[4] *The Servant of the Word* (New York: Charles Scribner's Sons, 1941), p. 116.

is more clearly expressed in Martin Arrowsmith's prayer:

> God give me unclouded eyes and freedom from haste. God give me a quiet and relentless anger against all pretense and all pretentious work and all work left slack and unfinished. God give me a restlessness whereby I may neither sleep nor accept praise till my observed results equal my calculated results or in pious glee I discover and assault my error. God give me strength not to trust to God! [5]

God seems to have answered the last petition. Many of our fellows seem to have the strength not to trust to God but to have limitless confidence in themselves. Yet, it would be wrong to assume that the American does this in a conscious, intellectual, thought-through fashion. Dr. Casserley says whimsically:

> It would be absurd to pretend that the average cheerful sabbath-breaker, at the cinema . . . or peacefully potting plants in his garden, has just read Darwin, Marx or Freud . . . He cares for none of these things. His conduct must be explained in terms of a pattern of life which he has inherited from his fathers. [6]

[5] Sinclair Lewis, *Arrowsmith* (New York: Harcourt, Brace and Company, 1925). The above quotation is taken from the Modern Library edition, pp. 280-281.

[6] J. V. L. Casserley, *The Retreat from Christianity in the Modern World* (New York: Longmans, 1952). Quoted in *Time*, December 29, 1952, p. 34.

He has entered into a comfortable existence, and he is sure it is the good life. Pragmatically, it is not going to be easy to disabuse him.

2. GENERAL NEIGHBORLINESS

There is a second aspect to the Word of the World, and that is the general neighborliness of America. I have never known anywhere else such a country of "joiners." Read the activities going on in any small town as listed in its weekly newspaper; it is a potpourri of group activities. (It is little wonder that group discussion is an American phenomenon, if not an American invention.) I discovered—almost to my horror—the other day that a church in Hollywood has 6,400 members and three hundred twenty-five different societies to which a member may belong.[7] (Thou hast made my Father's house a variegated and perpetual jamboree.) I can appreciate the worshipper who wrote the minister of one of New York's large churches in approbation, because no one had spoken to him in ten years of regular attendance, except the ushers, who said: "Good morning" and "Goodbye." Yet that is unfair. After all, the Church is a fellowship and not a casual collection of Lone Star Rangers. What must not

[7] *Time*, January 12, 1953, p. 55.

be forgotten is the American urge to be one of the gang, of many gangs, where the desire for neighborliness may be, and is, satisfied. I was told on leaving Scotland for this country that there was no home life in America. That is a lie. It is a country of porches; I found that as soon as I left New York for a small town in Pennsylvania, where I spent two summer months in 1928. Maybe the misinformation was due to the inevitable lack of porches in my native land. What use is a porch in Scotland, where it rains with a monotonous regularity which has to be endured to be believed? The porch-society of America is good, though I personally have never been able to break myself of the Scottish habit of staying indoors even in the balmiest weather. Yet, the unwillingness to be alone over here terrifies me. If, by mischance, one is left in solitariness, on goes the radio or television. While the cult of the juke box may be a sign of neighborliness, I am in agreement with the plea for a silent record, so that occasionally one may buy three minutes of quiet. Even then the instrument would remain lit up like the main street of Reno as an illuminated reminder of the shared noise to come.

This genuine, even affectionate, neighborliness has appeared in another guise in more recent days. There is a growing sense of interdependence which is enlarging our more local neighborliness. This was partly due to the war when New Englanders were trained in Georgia and where, sooner or later, everyone landed in Texas. It is not quite so easy to be "a Virginian, a Democrat and an Episcopalian, thank God," when the daughter in the family is happily married to a Unitarian who went to Harvard and votes Republican, while the son is the husband of a girl from Denver who attends the Community Church and is quite independent in her political views. Regionalism is on its way out as a cultural entity. Moreover such organizations as the Community Chest are bringing Negroes and Whites into a working partnership where one may more objectively assess the abilities and outlook of the "other" race. The central European races crowd the Irish off the Notre Dame team and, as Mr. Allen points out, in the World Series of 1950 Woodling, Rizzuto, Berra, DiMaggio, Mize, Brown, Bauer, Coleman and Raschi were all Yankees! [8]

When one seeks the "why" of this general neighborliness the answer is not easy to find. Is it a spiritual hangover from the Christian faith which once controlled our outlook? Though we are not as conscious of our vertical relationship to a God of love, we are still convinced of the need for and the value of a brotherly horizontal relationship to an ever-widening circle of our

[8] Allen, *op. cit.*, p. 206.

fellowmen. We are not only naturally gregarious; we are really desirous of community. Again to quote Allen —a most quotable man—"If we as a people do not obey the first and great commandment as numerously and fervently as we used to, at least we have been doing fairly well with the second." [9] He is right. I know from personal experience the fact of general neighborliness in this country.

3. ULTIMATE ANXIETY

There is a third aspect of this Word of the World which influences the members in our churches. It is quite different from the others, almost contradictory to the first, but as manifest when folk begin to reveal the deeper longings of their hearts and to unburden their souls. This is an underlying uneasiness of mind respecting the meaning of life and the outcome of their individual existences. It is an ever-present, if often latent, anxiety, an insecurity which appears as the "Hamlet cramp" when one thinks of what to do with his life, even more, when one tries to figure out what he is meant to be. It is partly caused by memory. The remembrance of the Great Depression of the early thirties makes us wonder if the present economic prosperity can last and if it does not, what then? It is partly caused by the threat

[9] *Ibid.*, p. 267.

of war, irritated by the seemingly long stalemate in Korea and the dread of the atomic and hydrogen bombs. It is due in some measure to the fact of responsibility on a scale that even Americans are not used to. To be one of two world powers, with the democratic segment looking to us for leadership, when we neither want it nor are ready for it, means that we stand apprehensively at the plate, in a real World Series, with two strikes already called against us. And beneath and behind and before all these worries is the certain promise of death. The farther it is pushed away by medical science the dearer life becomes; yet the fact is still there beckoning. No wonder man says "Whew! Let's skip it. Eat, drink and be merry, for tomorrow, if we're lucky, we may still eat, drink and be merry. Let's forget death." But he cannot. His father comes down with cancer; his son is killed in an auto accident, and his young brother is mortally wounded in Korea. He is pervaded with a sense of futility, of transience, of personal insignificance. He longs for a real sense of security; he wants to know that he counts for something and will always, hereafter as well as here, count for something. When he begins to be hopeful, because of a sound digestion or a good business deal or a satisfactory home life, some expert writes an article which scares him anew. Think of the devastation that Sir Charles Galton Darwin created at the Mount Holyoke College Convocation on *Science and Human Values* in the Fall of 1952. The official report of the meeting states that his address "stirred wide and spirited discussion and prompted one of the next day's speakers . . . to sit up late and revise his prepared talk so as to make a rejoinder." The two speeches are printed in a special insert. What was it that so upset many of these eight hundred listeners "including scientists, industrialists, and leaders in the humanities and education"? Here is an excerpt:

> The past history of the human race on our earth may be very loosely described as most of the time having been an untidy mess, and I see no reason whatever to expect that it will be different for most of the future time . . . My general conclusion about the future of the world then is that it will be like the past. There will be a perpetual struggle for means of subsistence, and in many parts of the world there will be people starving because not enough food can be produced for them . . . It is prosperity that is the abnormal condition and it would take—enormously more —than a little good sense for it to be extended over the rest of the world. In saying this I am leaving aside the question which I regard as extremely doubtful, whether the human race on the whole has the necessary good sense.[10]

[10] *The Convocation, Science and Human Values. A Pictorial Review.* (Published by Mount Holyoke College, 1952. No page numbers.) Reprinted by permission of Sir Charles G. Darwin.

How does the thoughtful man in the street react to that?
He may become an Ecclesiastes:

> Vanity of vanities; all is vanity . . . The thing that hath
> been, it is that which shall be; and that which is done is
> that which shall be done; and there is no new thing under the
> sun. . . . I have seen all the works that are done under the
> sun; and, behold, all is vanity and vexation of spirit.
>
> (1:2, 9, 14)

Or, he may nod assent to Edwin Arlington Robinson's
"Richard Cory": [11] Do you recall him?

> Whenever Richard Cory went down town,
> We people on the pavement looked at him;
> He was a gentleman from sole to crown,
> Clean favored, and imperially slim.
>
> And he was always quietly arrayed,
> And he was always human when he talked;
> But still he fluttered pulses when he said,
> "Good morning," and he glittered when he walked.
>
> And he was rich—yes, richer than a king—
> And admirably schooled in every grace:
> In fine, we thought that he was everything
> To make us wish that we were in his place.

[11] Reprinted from *The Children of the Night* by Edwin Arlington
Robinson, 1897; reprinted by permission of Charles Scribner's Sons.

So on we worked, and waited for the light,
And went without the meat, and cursed the bread;
And Richard Cory, one calm summer night,
Went home and put a bullet through his head.

There is, even where we would not suspect it, an ultimate anxiety.

It is, as we said, impossible to write a universally acceptable statement of the Word of the World. But in our American milieu we have caught something of its emphases: a pragmatic assurance, a general neighborliness, and an ultimate anxiety.

* * * * * *

Though characteristic of the World, we must remember that these viewpoints are in the Church. They are in the pulpit, because the preacher is a man in the World, affected by its interests and its outlook. They are in the pew, because we have been thinking not of the man of the World who stays away from the Church but of the man of the World whose name is on the ecclesiastical rolls. That man comes to church. It might be said that, at the middle of the century, he is coming back to church. That is witnessed to by the titles of contemporary novels; by the added courses in religion in numerous colleges; by the increase in the figures of church membership.

Let us look, then, at this man of the World or from the World in the Church, the nominal Christian. He has to be taken into account because by his presence or by his financial contribution he has something to say about what goes on in the Church. He may not be a pillar, but he is—as one such waggishly described himself— a flying buttress, one who supports from the outside. That he supports is important, because it means that he influences the mind of the Church. There he is, then, a man of four primary interests. He is bound up in his family to whom he wishes to give the best he can. He probably spoils his family; he may even intend to. One such father confessed to me, "What's the use of being a father if you can't spoil your children?". Another admitted that he willingly relinquished first claim on the family car to his only boy. Such behavior may make it difficult for that kind of a man to grasp what Jesus meant by the fatherhood of God in first century Jewish terms. Again, he is vitally interested in his job which gives him the wherewithal to maintain his home. He knows that an American job is a good one in point of hours and wages. It may not last; that is a worry. But he shakes his head at the biblical idea that work may be a curse, a penalty for sin. Thirdly, he loves his country. No wonder! It may be that I as a naturalized citizen know better how favorable a land these United States

are than one who was born into it. I come from a good
country, yet I appreciate what a "Promised Land" America is. If that is true for one from Scotland, consider
what America must mean to one from Latvia or Greece
or Italy. His heart beats faster when he thinks of
Washington and Jefferson, of Lincoln and Lee, of Wilson
and even of Roosevelt. In the last place, he enjoys his
contacts. He has an *esprit de corps* about his fellow
workers, about his civic club and lodge, about the ath-
letic teams, college and professional, which he backs.
They all give him a sense of community, of belonging
to something worthwhile. It may be true that General
Motors or the First National Bank is not the Kingdom
of God; that Rotarians and Elks fall short of the beloved community; that sport, rather than religion, is
the opiate of the people. But he enjoys them. "What
harm do they do?", he asks, knowing that they do much
good.

Culturally he admits he isn't very bright, despite
his B.A. or B.S. He knows that he spends too much time
with the *Saturday Evening Post* and *The Reader's Digest*
and *Time* and the sports columnists. But he subscribes
to the local symphony orchestra; he knows the name of
Walter Lippmann as well as of Yogi Berra; and, if
there is no football game being broadcast, he will at

least keep quiet while his wife listens to the Metropolitan Opera on Saturday afternoons in winter.

He is a traditionalist in all sorts of ways. He believes in the old-fashioned virtues, by which he means hard work, honesty in personal contacts, and independence. He is politically more or less what his father was and isn't over-enthusiastic about new deals and government interference and entangling alliances, unless he is benefited by them.

He thinks emotionally about community problems. He is concerned about the Negro as a brother-in-law rather than as a Christian brother or as a democratic neighbor. He is not quite sure where the Jew should live, but it shouldn't be in his neighborhood. He guesses that it may be all right for some folk to be Roman Catholics, but he is glad he isn't.

Yet he is a sentimentalist. He wants the minister to speak on behalf of race cooperation, and better relations between capital and labor, and higher ethical standards in government, provided it is all done in generalizations with no specific application. He will pray the General Confession but would rather the minister did not specify too particularly current sins in the other prayers. He constantly believes that one more war will solve everything, and cannot understand how the Kaiser could be succeeded by Mussolini and Hitler, and both be followed by Stalin and Malenkov.

He doesn't really know very much about Christianity, beyond a bed-time prayer, the simpler Bible stories and a few key verses. Of course, he doesn't know very much about anything outside his home, and his business, and the income tax returns. If you were to quiz him on American history, the Revolution would be a compilation of tea and Valley Forge and the Star Spangled Banner. The Civil War would be a concatenation of John Brown's Body and *Uncle Tom's Cabin,* General Grant's Whisky, the *Gettysburg Address,* Marching Through Georgia, and his grandfather's sword. He is not so much wrong as limitedly accurate.

Perhaps you have not seen the examination paper on the Christian faith which Dorothy L. Sayers compiled for her young English friends and the kind of answers that might be expected:

Q.: What does the Church think of God the Father?
A.: He is omnipotent and holy. He created the world and imposed on man conditions impossible of fulfillment; He is very angry if these are not carried out. He sometimes interferes by means of arbitrary judgments and miracles, distributed with a good deal of favouritism. He likes to be truckled to and is always ready to pounce on anybody who trips over a difficulty in the

Law, or is having a bit of fun. He is rather like a dictator, only larger and more arbitrary.

Q.: What does the Church think of God the Son?

A.: He is in some way to be identified with Jesus of Nazareth. It was not His fault that the world was made like this, and, unlike God the Father, He is friendly to man and did His best to reconcile man to God . . . He has a good deal of influence with God, and if you want anything done, it is best to apply to Him.

Q.: What does the Church think of God the Holy Ghost?

A.: I don't know exactly. He was never seen or heard of till Whit-Sunday. There is a sin against Him which damns you for ever, but nobody knows what it is.

Q.: What is the doctrine of the Trinity?

A.: 'The Father incomprehensible, the Son incomprehensible, and the whole thing incomprehensible.' Something put in by theologians to make it more difficult— nothing to do with daily life or ethics.

Q.: What was Jesus Christ like in real life?

A.: He was a good man—so good as to be called the Son of God. He is to be identified in some way with God the Son. He was meek and mild and preached a simple religion of love and pacifism. He had no sense of humour. Anything in the Bible that suggests another side to His character must be an interpolation, or a paradox invented by G. K. Chesterton. If we try to live like Him, God the Father will let us off being damned hereafter and only have us tortured in this life instead.

Q.: What is meant by the Atonement?
A.: God wanted to damn everybody, but His vindictive sadism was sated by the crucifixion of His own Son, who was quite innocent, and, therefore, a particularly attractive victim. He now only damns people who don't follow Christ or who never heard of Him.

Q.: What does the Church think of sex?
A.: God made it necessary to the machinery of the world and tolerates it, provided the parties (a) are married, and (b) get no pleasure out of it.

Q.: What does the Church call Sin?
A.: Sex (otherwise than as excepted above); getting drunk; saying 'damn'; murder, and cruelty to dumb animals; not going to church; most kinds of amusement. 'Original sin' means that anything we enjoy doing is wrong.

Q.: What is faith?
A.: Resolutely shutting your eyes to scientific fact.

Q.: What is the human intellect?
A.: A barrier to faith.

Q.: What are the seven Christian virtues?

A.: Respectability; childishness; mental timidty; dullness; sentimentality; censoriousness; and depression of spirits.

Q.: Wilt thou be baptized in this faith?
A.: No fear! [12]

Now, like my delineation of the man of the World in the Church, that is overdrawn. It is caricature. But there is enough truth in it to make us realize that he must be spoken to about the Faith simply, intelligently and constantly. The job is one of education, and since Sunday morning is almost the only chance we have to talk to and with such a person more and more emphasis will have to be put on the teaching sermon. Our next step is to link the Word of God and the man of the World in the Church in such a way that the result is still the Word of God but one which interests, upsets and lays hold on the nominal Christian.

[12] *Creed or Chaos?* (New York: Harcourt Brace, 1949), pp. 21-23.

IV

The Word and the Words of the Preacher

WITH that long but necessary analysis of the Word of God and the Word of the World behind us, we are ready to direct our attention to the actual composition of the sermon. Here, then, is a minister sitting down at his desk and preparing himself to introduce some aspect of the Christian World-view to his congregation. He must subconsciously keep both in mind, the subject and the listener.

Where is he to begin, with the Word of God or with the human situation? It makes no difference, so far as content is concerned, provided he remembers that he must deal with the other also before he words his sermon. Let us assume he has decided to start with the Christian World-view as it is enshrined in a section of Scripture.

He piles on his desk several translations of the Bible, a concordance and two or three commentaries. He has, close by, books on biblical history and literature. He concentrates on a passage which reveals to him and, he hopes, to his congregation the Word of God. He knows that there are three complementary ways of tearing the truth out of the text. The first is through a comparison of the multiple translations in English, and in other languages if the native tongues are dumb for him. The second is through exegesis: the critical analysis of the selected verses in their geographical, historical and cultural settings, with special attention paid to the author's purpose. The third is through exposition: the elucidation of the spiritual principle in the passage as it is determined by the exegesis.

One reason why there is general rejoicing at the appearance of *The Interpreter's Bible* is that it makes use of these three ways of construing Scripture.[1] At the top of each page are set side by side the King James Version and the Revised Standard Version. They should remind us that Goodspeed and Moffatt and Weymouth and others may be of help also. In the middle of the page is the Exegesis, the work of able biblical scholars. Below the Exegesis is the Exposition, theoretically based on the Exegesis, the production of men who are assumed

[1] See p. 41.

to be pulpit masters. In addition, there are Introductions and General Articles, Maps and Indexes. We are debtors to the Abingdon-Cokesbury Press for publishing such a commentary. He is a wise divider of the Word of God who will read and learn by heart the suggestions in "How to Use the Interpreter's Bible" in the first volume.[2]

This part of the preparation is work. It means digging, and turning over, and sifting the passage to find the real Word of God. It is imperative that he first discern and then discount the local and temporal, so that what is eternal, and therefore permanent, may stand alone. Even when that is done, the sermon is not yet ready to be worded, far less preached. Now the minister must clear his desk of the accumulated Bibles and commentaries, and in his mind's eye visualize his congregation to whose advantage he is going to expound this Word. What do they look like? What are they busy at in the World? What kind of folk make up his flock? It is not enough to see them as plumbers and store clerks and income tax collectors; as stenographers and housewives and old maids; as professors, firemen and Pullman porters. He must picture them more individually. There is a waitress who, poor soul, chronically suffers from hay fever, and a night watchman who understandably

[2] Pp. xvii-xxi.

goes to sleep during the sermon. There is a widow and her three neatly dressed children who never miss the eleven o'clock service, and a man who always comes alone because his wife is a Roman Catholic. There is a college boy who is present during the vacations, but only because he is under the discipline of home. It is a motley company of men and women who traffic and market in the streets of the World, who find much of their amusement and recreation there, who are renters of houses and builders of homes, and who come to church—sometimes, often, regularly. Them he must see. He must smile at them, and nod to them, and talk with them as he mulls over his sermon. He must know them, really know them. That is why pastoral visitation is a *sine qua non* of helpful preaching.

So the preparer of the sermon, at this point, has to reverse his field. He has been pulling the eternal out of the temporary; now he must do the opposite. He must insert the timeless Word into time—his time, their time, contemporary time. He must surround the World-view with the twentieth century, in his parish. He must paint the Word with local colour. This, too, is work. The good exegete may fail completely when it comes to application in a given situation. I think of one able theological professor who, on being told that his sermonic ideas were sound but that the congregation couldn't grasp their significance, remarked: "Damn the congregation." Why does he bother to write a sermon? It is for their sake that we do all this exegesis and exposition. Otherwise we shall be voices crying in an ecclesiastical wilderness, where even the echoes are hardly heard in the world. Think of it in this way. What is the meaning of the Incarnation? Is it not that God, realizing that man did not (could not) apprehend Him in His essential being, had to clothe Himself in a form which could be grasped by ordinary folk? Is the Word of God so very different? If our interpretation of it is correct, then the Word is known only as it is seen, understood and remembered because of a historical occurrence or person. How then can our people appreciate its import for them if all we do in a sermon is to free it from its ancient historical trappings? We must re-clothe it for today. We must re-set it in an up-to-date mounting. The eternal Word must become a contemporary Word (with a capital W) through conscious, direct, specific application. It is when the minister sees the Christian World-view penetrating an immediately relevant human situation that a sermon is born.

Think of our Lord. Part of his secret in arresting the multitudes was that he was able to house the things of heaven amid the furniture of earth. God was seen in the attitude of a Palestinian father toward a run-away boy who came home, maybe back to Nazareth. Love was illustrated by the behavior of a Samaritan to his historic enemy, a Jew. The gracious outgoing of the Word of God was pictured in the analogy of a shepherd hunting for a sheep which had become separated from the flock. No wonder the common people followed him in droves. It would not be unwise for the disciple to learn from his master. Have you heard of Brother Bryant, the beloved minister of Birmingham, Alabama, who was so dear to the heart of his fellow citizens that they erected a statue of him while he was still living? He kept practically no worldly possessions but a shelter over his head, the clothes he stood in and two books. Do you know what the books were? The Bible and the telephone directory. One kept him in touch with God, the other with man. He would have been less effective, if not ineffective, with either, alone. He drew inspiration as he lifted up his eyes to God; he drew relevance as he turned them to men. So with us. We may not be able to build Jerusalem in "England's green and pleasant land" or along the marshes of the Potomac; but we should see Jacob's Ladder set up between heaven and Charing Cross and Harvard Square and Five Points.

This linking of the Word of God and the man of the World may be clarified if we sketch briefly the content of three sermons. We shall not discuss the parts of the sermon: Introduction, Body, Conclusion; nor shall we seek to discover the various moulds into which the stuff of the sermon may be run. We want to see the contemporary Word of the Preacher in three human situations.

What shall the preacher say about the pragmatic assurance of our time—the cult of self-dependability and the materialistic yard-stick for measuring all things? He could start from the parable of the Rich Fool (Luke 12:16-21) and tackle the matter biographically. But he wants to deal with it as the prevailing national attitude rather than as focused in an individual. Amos can help him. He lived in an age of unprecedented prosperity in the Northern Kingdom under Jeroboam II. Amos was energetically outraged with the by-products of such worldly comfort: the callousness and immorality of the rich and the degradation and despoiling of the poor. Here are two extracts:

> Woe to those who are at ease in Zion,
> and to those who feel secure on the mountain of
>   Samaria,
> the notable men of the first of the nations,
> to whom the house of Israel come!
>
> Woe to those who lie upon beds of ivory,
> and stretch themselves upon their couches,
> and eat lambs from the flock,

and calves from the midst of the stall;
who sing idle songs to the sound of the harp,
and like David invent for themselves instruments of
    music;
who drink wine in bowls,
and anoint themselves with the finest oils,
but are not grieved over the ruin of Joseph!
                        (Amos 6:1, 4-6)

Hear this, you who trample upon the needy,
and bring the poor of the land to an end,
saying, "When will the new moon be over,
that we may sell grain?
And the sabbath,
that we may offer wheat for sale,
that we may make the ephah small and the shekel
    great,
and deal deceitfully with false balances,
that we may buy the poor for silver
and the needy for a pair of sandals,
and sell the refuse of the wheat?"
                        (Amos 8:4-6)

As he discerns the Word of God, the moral outcome can be only judgment, judgment which involves national punishment on no small scale:

The high places of Isaac shall be made desolate, and the sanctuaries of Israel shall be laid waste, and I will rise against the house of Jeroboam with the sword.

                        (Amos 7:9)

So far so good, but the end of the sermon is not yet. He now must find a parallel in our time, not merely a succession of wicked incidents, but an atmosphere of man-centeredness. Can he? Let him read Herbert Butterfield's *Christianity and History* [3] and Reinhold Niebuhr's *The Irony of American History* [4] and Arnold Toynbee's *A Study of History*.[5] They will bring him up to date with what happens to a nation which believes that life consisteth in the abundance of the things which it hath, much of it taken by force from others. Part of the true Word of God is judgment. But let him preach it for America rather than for Russia. Perhaps the closing hymn should be Kipling's "Recessional."

What will he say about the general friendliness of our contemporaries? He will be glad of it and let his people know he is glad; it is good to live with neighborly people. This may be the place for a key-word study. Let him, with the help of Nygren [6] and Kittel,[7] examine the New Testament idea of "Love" (*agapé*). He will find that it is not general neighborliness. It does

[3] New York: Charles Scribner's Sons, 1950.

[4] New York: Charles Scribner's Sons, 1952.

[5] New York: Oxford University Press (Abridged edition), 1947.

[6] Anders Nygren, *Agape and Eros*, Translated by A. G. Herbert (New York: The Macmillan Company, 1932).

[7] *Bible Key Words* from Gerhard Kittel's *Theologisches Wörterbuch zum Neuen Testament*. Translated and edited by J. R. Coates (New York: Harper and Brothers, 1951).

not necessarily involve liking a person. It is good will or genuine respect, and is the result of thinking God's thoughts after him. He was the kind of God who gathered together the outcasts of Israel according to the Psalmist (147:2). Jesus said that behavior like God's involved more than loving those who loved you (Matthew 5:46). What plus is there to that? Christian love embraces those not usually embraced; it goes out to those who cannot offer a *quid pro quo*. Modern illustrations for this are easy to find, but the one who struggles with this topic would do well to remember that in preaching it he had better be humble. Our behavior in church and across denominational lines is hardly an example to the World of Christian love in flaming action. When I see the World (for its own reasons) accept Negroes on baseball teams and as café entertainers, I sometimes shudder to think that two of the last strongholds of white supremacy in the U.S.A. will be the small denominational college and the local church. There is judgment as well as mercy in love as a Word of God.

How will he tackle his third sermon, on the anxiety of the World? He can hardly open his Bible without finding a Word of reassurance and encouragement. Isaiah and Second Isaiah trumpet it; it is broadcast repeatedly in the Psalms. But if he wants to deal with the answer in a biographical manner, let him read right through one of the Gospels, non-stop. Let him steep himself in this passage from the Sermon on the Mount:

> Therefore I tell you, do not be anxious about your life, what you shall eat or what you shall drink, nor about your body, what you shall put on. Is not life more than food, and the body more than clothing? Look at the birds of the air: they neither sow nor reap nor gather into barns, and yet your heavenly Father feeds them. Are you not of more value than they? And which of you by being anxious can add one cubit to his span of life? And why are you anxious about clothing? Consider the lilies of the field, how they grow; they neither toil nor spin; yet I tell you, even Solomon in all his glory was not arrayed like one of these. But if God so clothes the grass of the field, which today is alive and tomorrow is thrown into the oven, will he not much more clothe you, O men of little faith?
>
> (MATTHEW 6:25-30)

Let him recall that if, for a moment, Jesus seemed to be overwhelmed with anxiety on the Cross, he rallied, gave comfort to a criminal alongside him, and committed himself to the care of God. And do not forget the Resurrection and its promise to us—the ultimate answer to ultimate anxiety. If the Crucifixion shows us the love of God in Christ, the Resurrection reveals the power of God in the face of the last enemy, which is death. It was the Resurrection which Paul preached primarily; the Christian hope is the climactic note of the New Testament. Turgeniev's Liza was right when she said: "One must be a Christian . . . not in order to recognize what is heavenly, or what is earthly, but because everyone must die." The risen Christ, the first fruits of them that rise, is the individual and personal answer to Korea and terminal cancer and death-dealing calamity. Someone has wisely said that the Reformation stressed faith, and the social gospel emphasized love, and it was time that we recaptured the note of hope.

There, then, is the Word of the Preacher, which is the Word of God to the Word of the World in our day.

* * * * * *

But we are not finished with the preparation of the sermon. Having puzzled out the message and placed it in the context of the hearer, the minister must now find words in which to couch it. The next step is that of "Communication," the delivery of his thinking from the study and the pulpit to the pew. He must "word" his Word. This is partly a matter of verbal expression, so let me spend the rest of this chapter on two facts to be kept in mind as one is phrasing the thought of the sermon. Let us turn from the Word of the Preacher to the words of the preacher.

THE WORD AND THE WORDS OF THE PREACHER

1. VOCABULARY

Let us look first at the preacher's vocabulary. Use words which the congregation understands. Article XXIV of the Thirty-nine Articles reads:

It is a thing plainly repugnant to the Word of God, and the custom of the Primitive Church, to have public Prayer in the Church, or to minister the Sacraments, in a tongue not understanded of the people.

The reference is to the Roman Catholic use of Latin in the liturgy, but allow a Presbyterian to add a rider:

It is also a thing plainly repugnant to the Word of God, if not to the custom of the Primitive Church, to use *pulpiteese* in the sermon, a tongue not understanded of the people.

The days of bewildered adoration before what is happening in the pulpit have largely gone. A hundred years ago that may not have been true. A Scottish woman on hearing Dr. Chalmers preach is said to have remarked to a neighbor: "That was a magnificent sermon." On being asked if she understood it, she indignantly replied: "Understand it! I wouldn't presume to understand it." Most of us are not Chalmers and will not receive such ignorant adulation, though some of us do receive more than we deserve. Therefore it behooves us to be understandable.

We have as much right as the other professions to use technical terms, but we must define them. It is foolish of us, inured to three years of theological discipline, to forget that the listeners have not undergone such exposure. Do you recall the cartoon—in *Punch*, I think—of the baffled congregation looking vacantly at the preacher as he bellows: "Ha! You will say that this savors of Sabellianism." What does the average American congregation know about Sabellianism, unless it happens to be the name of a horse that ran in the Kentucky Derby or a football player in the Notre Dame backfield? Yet Sabellianism is a common heresy, a reasonable heresy. Perhaps the only way in which the Doctrine of the Trinity can be made homiletically comprehensible is in terms of Sabellianism: three manifestations, three aspects of the one God in His relation to man as Creator, Incarnate Redeemer and Sanctifier. God is one person as well as one substance. As one person He is indivisible, but He has three ways of operating. As creator and governor God is known as Father; as Redeemer He is named the Son; as Regenerator and Sanctifier He is called the Holy Spirit. But He is always one and the same God. The difference is in function. Is that clear? Of course it isn't. But at least we have tried to say what it meant. It will not be clear until the Doctrine of the Trinity is "applied" to our contemporary life. Then we shall probably be Sabellians and on the threshold of a heresy trial! Do not be afraid to define, to repeat the definition, to spell it out, to go over it. Where the besetting sin of the old preacher is the prevalence of cliché, that of the young preacher is "gobbledegook" or "bafflegab." (Cliché is often superannuated gobbledegook.) Let me explain. "Gobbledegook" or "bafflegab" is the name given to the excessive use of unexplained esoteric, departmental, technical language in communications to the general public. The temples of bafflegab are the agencies of the Federal governments; its high priests are civil servants. But it is not unknown in the professions. Within the expert group it is probably not only a harmless but a useful method of communicating. For theologians *agapé* and "realized eschatology" and *Heilsgeschichte* are valuable and valid time-savers in conversation. That is so because they have been defined carefully, discussed at length, and accepted generally. They are not to be used in the pulpit unless much care is given to definition and explanation. Many common theological terms are not intelligible to our congregations: Divided Kingdom, Babylonian Captivity, Post-exilic Prophecy, Son of Man, Synoptic Gospels, Hellenistic, Apostolic Age, Holy Ghost. Take that last term, Holy Ghost. It is connected in my mind with the story of the little girl who lived over the wall from a cemetery and who was, one day, observed in the act of burying her teddy bear. She stood over the hole which she had dug in the garden, with the bear in her hands, and gravely announced: "In the name of the Father, and of the Son, and in the hole he goes." That is the result of bafflegab. Cliché is a generally used, well-worn term which has lost any specific, clear-cut connotation for the hearer, like Lamb of God, Elder Brother (as applied to Jesus), Bread of Life, Atoning Death, Saved by Grace, Washed in the Blood. The idea in each is still sound, valid; but through too much useless use they have become flat, rubbed thin, meaningless.

Yet, congregations are willing to be instructed. Terms interest them. Definitions help them grasp ideas. Words do have specific content. Herb Caen, the columnist in the *San Francisco Examiner*, tells this story of a drunk, moaning and groaning in police court one morning. The judge asked him solicitously: "My good man, do you have a hangover?" The reply baffled the court: "No, Your Honor; me, I've got a holdover." He went on to explain: "There is a difference, see? You wake up sober, but feeling awful—that's a hangover. You wake up feeling awful, but still drunk—that's a holdover. I got a holdover." [8] That is the kind of careful distinction that we must make in our sermons. A dictionary and a thesaurus will be required reading throughout our lives. They will make us word conscious, and they should enliven our preaching. The unforgivable sin in a sermon is that it be dull, uninteresting, stolid and inert. Yet so many sermons are that. David Read, the Chaplain of Edinburgh University, has pointed out that one of the definitions of preaching in the *Oxford Dictionary* is: "to give moral or religious advice in an obtrusive or tiresome way." [9] Think of the generations of preaching which forced the editors of that dictionary to include such a definition. One way to avoid such a criticism of our preaching is to watch our vocabulary. The raw material of our preaching is old; it has been handed down for generations. We are interpreters of a tradition. Yet it is also eternal; therefore, it is always contemporary. Making it sound new is a matter of explanation and application of terms. The President of Duke University, commenting to me on a sermon preached by one of my colleagues, remarked: "I congratulated him on that sermon. For fifteen years I've been waiting for someone to make 'Justification by Faith' mean something for us

[8] Herb Caen, *Baghdad-By-The-Bay* (Garden City, New York: Doubleday & Company, 1949), pp. 69-70.

[9] *The Communication of the Gospel* (London: S.C.M. Press, 1952), p. 82.

today. He did it. I've heard many old-fashioned sermons on it; when they were finished all one carried away was the tone of the preacher's voice. This man made me know what 'Justification by Faith' was all about." How did the preacher manage to elicit such a response? He knew the content of the doctrine; he believed it; he defined it; he applied it; he used language that revealed rather than concealed the meaning. Therefore we must concentrate on vocabulary once we have laid hold on an idea and know the human situation in which it has to be turned to account.

2. ORAL STYLE

In the second place, remember that the sermon is to be heard by listeners in a church, not to be read by people from a book. You must therefore word your message in an oral style rather than in an essay style. This is not easy, especially if you write out your manuscript in full. Almost inevitably you will fall into the "read" style. What distinguishes an oral style? Let me stress three aspects.

1. It is conversational—dignified and vigorous—but conversational. We live in an age and a land where "the cult of informality is pervasive." [10]

10 Frederick Lewis Allen, *The Big Change* (New York: Harper and Brothers, 1952), p. 229.

Look at the way we dress as compared with fifty years ago. Look at the way we entertain.

Think of the words which describe our informal, unpretentious American living: blue jeans, cafeteria, juke box, square dance. The day of the oratorical sermon and the rhetorical sentence is passing, except as it is archaeologically preserved in an old-fashioned pulpiteer or an elderly senator. Of course, the sermon is not really a conversation; it is still a monologue, but it can be given the flavor of good conversation, and kept from monotony and absurdity. Make the sentences short. For a beginner it is wise never to write a sentence which takes more than one breath to deliver. This is not a plea for deep breathing, but for brief, pointed statements. Use many periods; some semi-colons; few commas; and no parentheses. Remember to repeat important ideas. If you were writing an essay this would not be as necessary; the reader could go back over your paragraphs, time and again, to find your central thought. But you are speaking and he is listening. Therefore, you must do his re-reading for him. So repeat, repeat, repeat. Re-define technical terms; stress key ideas; accent important words. This is particularly important if the general end of the sermon is to explain or to convince; and more and more of our sermons should be to explain or to convince. There is a place for good teaching from the pulpit.

In this conversational form of writing, make use of the "rhetorical question," that is, the question which is not intended to elicit an answer, but to create an attitude of interest and involvement on the part of the congregation. Make your listeners pay attention by asking such questions as: "If you had heard Jesus say to his disciples, 'Who do men say that I am?', what would you have answered?"; "If this were the last sermon you were to hear, what would you wish the minister to preach about?"; "If you were Secretary of State, how much Christianity would you hope to include in the nation's foreign policy?" That lassoes a listener; it pulls the congregation up with a jerk. It brings the hearer into the discussion as an involved participant. Let me enter one caveat: do not use the rhetorical question in the children's sermon. You may receive an answer which will knock you out of the pulpit. I heard of a rejoinder which kept a congregation off balance for the rest of the service. Let me tell it, because it carries a theological as well as a homiletical word to the wise. The minister was indulging in rhetorical question: "What is it that lives up a tree, has a furry body, a bushy tail, beady eyes and whiskers?" He received the audible answer: "God." The youthful responder was removed by his father from the church. At the door he asked his son this non-rhetorical question: "What on earth did you mean by saying that?" Can you guess the answer? "Oh, heck, I knew it was a squirrel. But he ought to be talking about God up there." Rhetorical question is a good device, except in the children's sermon.

2. In addition to being conversational, be simple. Remember that while you have spent from ten to twenty hours mulling over the idea you seek to express, the congregation has given no time to it, in all probability. Therefore, lead them gently but clearly into your thinking, and from place to place within it. Work hard on your transitions. Tell your listener when you move from your first point to your second, and from your second to your third. You know when you have made the transfer; assist them to make it with you. Do not be afraid to be obvious; if you can also be natural and graceful, so much the better.

Why is it that Dr. Fosdick is constantly quoted among Fundamentalists as a pulpit master? It is certainly not his theological point of view. Regarding that they are more ready to call him "anti-Christ." It is the sheer simplicity of his style. There is a directness, an understandability, a clarity, which marks his pulpit performance. His aim is not eloquence but communicability. He is limpid, but not shallow; penetrating, but not impertinent. He talks to us, not at us. Therefore, he is the master, even for the Fundamentalists, when it comes to the style (and the structure) of the sermon.

A distinguished American preacher once shared this confidence with me. He had listened to a theological lecture which by its erudition, its use of language, and its obscurity of style so bamboozled him that he left the convocation in a humiliated frame of mind. It was back to the farm for him, not even to milk cows, just to dig ditches. Then he rallied, and decided to stay in the ministry. He said that what resuscitated him were some words of Jesus: "Feed my lambs." Not "feed my giraffes" but "feed my lambs." He left the giraffes to the lecturer; he returned to the lambs. Be simple.

3. In the third place, in your oral expression, be picturesque. A good preacher makes the listeners do more than hear him. They see what he is describing. They smell it and taste it and touch it. A sermon should appeal to more senses than the ear. To this day I can, from my mother's description, picture John Hutton, later editor of *The British Weekly*, telling the story of Jonah and the whale. As he described Jonah's reaction to the storm, before he found some sort of a haven within the big fish, John Hutton's face turned green, and one wondered if he could keep from being seasick over the edge of the pulpit. That may be carrying things too far, but the intent is right. He knew the teaching power of nar-

rative. We are to tell the Word attractively, winningly, colorfully.

Therefore, we must watch our language. The poets will show us how to use the right word in the right place, if we will bother to analyze their sentences, seeking to change and improve on their choice of words. The able preacher will reveal to us part of his secret if we will count his adjectives and his adverbs, and realize how his strength lies in the verbs and the nouns first, and in the carefully chosen adjectives and adverbs second. We should never write without a thesaurus or even better *Webster's Dictionary of Synonyms* open beside us.[11] "Dredge" is a more picturesque word than "dig," and "somersault" than "inversion." "An agnostic who walks on tiptoe" is a more colorful phrase than "an unbeliever who isn't so sure."

When a minister stimulates our senses his message is more easily remembered. If you do not believe that, read Peter Marshall's sermons and you will change your mind.[12] Even his biblical characters are alive; they strut and slink across the stage; they remind us of the man next door and of the woman across the street. We see them; they see us. The effect of such picturesque speech

[11] Springfield (Mass.) : G. and C. Merriam Company, 1942.

[12] *Mr. Jones, Meet the Master* (New York: Fleming H. Revell Company, 1949).

was brought home to me on a sick visit. The patient confessed that he was living with another woman as well as with his wife. He added: "You won't believe this, but it is her cooking that pulls me away from home." Fumbling in my mind for the correct rejoinder, I stalled for time by suggesting he tell me about her cooking. He chose a simple dish—French fried potatoes. He described her preparing them: the sharp knife; the clean cutting; the bubbling fat; the golden, succulent, redolent result (I looked up these adjectives in the thesaurus). He awaited my reaction. With my taste buds working overtime, there was only one thing I could think of saying: "What's her address?". I managed to restrain myself, but with difficulty. I wished that his gift for description could be conferred on my students, and on me. Happy is the congregation whose preacher uses a picturesque oral style.

Is there any specific piece of study we can undertake to improve our vocabulary, to help us develop an oral style? Yes, there is one valuable discipline. Choose a great preacher who has allowed his sermons to be printed, who has delivered a series of published lectures on preaching, and who has been the subject of a biography—such men as P. T. Forsyth and J. H. Jowett. Study him for a year. Know him as a person; work with him on his sermons; master his preaching methods. Do not imitate him, but keep asking yourself: What has he to teach me about living and thinking and writing and speaking? Next year study another. Do the same for a poet, especially one who has published his theory of poetry. And keep remembering that what you learn has to be applied in your parish by you. Do not read sermons for ideas or illustrations. That is the easy descent to the homiletical Avernus. Buy volumes of sermons sparingly, and use them with great discretion.

* * * * * *

It is not an easy task to which we are called. It is a mental and spiritual work-out to impart the Word of God, in love, to the church member who is perforce making a daily compromise with the World. It demands the head and the heart working together, and the communication of their findings in words which sound sensible and make sense. The most difficult period in our ministry is not when we begin, but twenty years after. Then the steady grind of the study, of the pulpit and the parish wearies the flesh, tires the mind and hardens the heart. At such a time Rudyard Kipling has some wisdom for us:

As the day wears, and the impetus of the morning dies away, there will come upon you an overwhelming sense of the uselessness of your toil. This must be striven against, and the only spur in your side will be the belief that you are playing against the Devil for the living soul.[13]

We are playing for God against the Devil in the World for the living soul, our own and those committed to our care. But God is with us. That is the partnership which sends us back to the struggle refreshed, back to the study and to the parish, to find the Word and the words of the Preacher.

[13] From "The Judgment of Dungara," in *In Black and White* (New York: Charles Scribner's Sons, 1898), p. 48.

V

The Word in the Believer

WHEN a minister delivers a sermon from the pulpit
to the pew, what is he trying to do? Granted that
he has pored over the words of the Bible until he has
found the Word of God, and granted that he has managed to link it with the man from the World, what is he
up to in the sermon? Theoretically he is proclaiming
that a person may be in good relations with God if he
desires it. Is that all? No. He is also instructing the believer how to stay in good relations with God. Well, is
that all? No. He is, in addition, summoning the believer
to allow the active Word of God to become effective in
the contemporary world through him. Preaching, then,
is a combination of announcement and teaching and
stimulus. We do the kind of work outlined in the previous
chapters so that the listener may become a believer, a
disciple, and an apostle. We preach that the Word of
God may become flesh again.

Before the minister may with integrity seek that end, it is necessary that he himself be the kind of person he desires his hearers to become. Therefore, let us consider the preacher as a believer, the believer he should be before he talks about the things of God to others.

There are some verses from Second Corinthians which should be engraved in every minister's heart. In them Paul brings to focus the preacher's blessed task and arduous privilege. Here they are:

> If any one is in Christ, he is a new creation; the old has passed away, behold, the new has come. All this is from God, who through Christ reconciled us to himself and gave us the ministry of reconciliation.
>
> (II CORINTHIANS 5:17-18)

Just in case the Corinthians could not grasp that, Paul said it all over again:

> That is, God was in Christ reconciling the world to himself, not counting their trespasses against them, and entrusting to us the message of reconciliation.
>
> (II CORINTHIANS 5:19)

And, lest there were yet some who were "slow in the uptak'," he adds:

> So we are ambassadors for Christ, God making his appeal through us.
>
> (II CORINTHIANS 5:20)

If we were to ask Paul how any man could take on such a job, he would answer us, as he once wrote the Galatians:

> I have been crucified with Christ; it is no longer I who live, but Christ who lives in me . . .
>
> (GALATIANS 2:20)

Do not imagine that Paul's character and personality were completely displaced by the indwelling Christ. In the rest of that verse he is quite ego-conscious:

> . . . and the life I now live in the flesh I live by faith in the Son of God, who loved me and gave himself for me.

He is Christ-possessed, not self-obliterated. It is a matter of re-incarnation. As the Word became flesh in Jesus of Nazareth, it again becomes flesh in Paul of Tarsus. It is because of that dispossession of the outlook of the "old man" to the Christian World-view as evidenced in Jesus of Nazareth, who lived, died, was raised by the power of God and takes possession of the believer, that Paul was able to say flatly to the Corinthians:

> But we have the mind of Christ.
>
> (I CORINTHIANS 2:16)

and to the Philippians:

> Have this mind among yourselves, which you have in Christ Jesus.
>
> (PHILIPPIANS 2:5)

Paul's experience is hardly normative, but he expected it to be. For us to be ambassadors, accredited ministers, we must know what he knew from personal experience. Before we can preach the Word as effectively as we should, we must be the Word re-incarnated. It should be for us "nae carried story." We must have had the kind of first-hand encounter with God which will empower us to say, as Job was enabled to say:

> I had heard of thee by the hearing of the ear,
> but now my eye sees thee;
> therefore I despise myself
> and repent in dust and ashes.
>
> (JOB 42:5-6)

With the repentance there comes the realization of God's good will. For us also there comes the commission to be His minister. When we have discovered for ourselves the Word of God bringing us into good relations with Him, then we are ready to be made ready to preach the message of reconciliation.

Therefore, before the minister ever enters the pulpit his life is a sermon, the Word of God become flesh. Because Paul knew that, he said on more than one occasion words which have offended some of his spiritually timid readers. To the Corinthians he wrote:

> Be imitators of me.　(I CORINTHIANS 11:1)

He immediately added "as I am of Christ." The only way many folk can set eyes upon Christ is to recognize him in a Christian. If the man of the World does not see Christ in the preacher outside of his pulpit, it is not likely that he will hear Christ when the preacher is in the pulpit. This fact is so important for F. C. Porter of Yale that he writes: "One who cannot say, Be imitators of me as I am of Christ, is not Christian." [1]

Yes, the Word of God is our message, but the message is best transmitted by the behavior of the minister. That is why Broadus in the Introduction to his volume on preaching lists "piety" as the first requisite of effective preaching.[2] That is why James Black of Edinburgh on hearing, during a game of golf, a younger clergyman address his ball in vehement terms, remarked: "Steady. Remember you are always on duty." That is why A. J. Gossip wrote of Alexander Cumming of Forfar:

> As the tall, stooping, venerable figure moved about the streets, pausing to pet a bairn, or slipping up a close on yet another of the endless little kindnesses with which he crowded the happy days, faces everywhere lit up at the sight

[1] *The Mind of Christ in Paul* (New York: Charles Scribner's Sons, 1932), p. 32.

[2] John A. Broadus, *On the Preparation and Delivery of Sermons* (New York: Harper and Brothers, copyright 1870; revised 1944), p. 6.

of him; and people, their voices suddenly grown softer, became kindlier in conversation when he hove in sight.[3]

Think of the ministers who mean much to you. Aren't they, with rare exceptions, men of the type of Alexander Cumming, whose whole life said: "Be imitators of me as I am of Christ"? It was not primarily that he preached good sermons; he was a sermon. It is hard, if not impossible, for a Christless man to preach Christ. It is hard, if not impossible, for a Christ-possessed man not to preach Christ, in the pulpit and out of it.

The highest tribute I ever read to this fact, this necessary fact, of re-incarnation was paid to Dr. J. H. Jowett. A popular magazine was anxious to discover why he packed the Fifth Avenue Presbyterian Church in New York. It sent one of its ablest writers to discover the secret of Jowett's drawing power. His report was something as follows:

I could not determine where the secret of Dr. Jowett's power over his people lay. It could not have been in his oratorical manner, for he had none; he read every word of his address, and his voice was slightly monotonous. He made almost no gestures, but stood practically motionless behind his pulpit desk. What most impressed me, I think, was that the longer Dr. Jowett spoke the less his audience was con-

[3] *In Christ's Stead* (London: Hodder and Stoughton, 1925), p. 79.

scious that he was there at all. He seemed gradually to disappear, and it took no great imagination to feel that instead of Jowett standing there, the Christ concerning whom he spoke stood in his place.[4]

That is an awesome standard.

Before we dare enter the pulpit, God's Word must have so penetrated our character that we live by it and for it in our daily walk and conversation. For that is the kind of preacher people wish to see and to hear. They watch him talk about what he is. They believe in the Incarnate Word because they see the Word re-incarnate in their minister, so they understand that God never leaves Himself without a witness in any age.

Let me introduce you to such a man today, to my own father-in-God, Henry Sloane Coffin. Here is how an Episcopalian has sketched him in the pulpit for us:

When therefore—to come from the general to the particular—one thinks of Henry Sloane Coffin, one remembers instantly certain flashing characteristics of his look and manner, and yet at the same moment knows that these are only tokens of something more important. The tall spare figure in the black Geneva gown with the white bands at the throat, the quick expressive hands, the fine-cut mobile face with its lifting eyebrows, the incisive speech with its Ameri-

[4] Frank S. Hickman, "Protestant Preaching at the Cross-Roads," *The Duke School of Religion Bulletin*, Vol. I, No. 1 (February 1936), p. 6.

can vigor and with some of the Scotch over-tones caught in Edinburgh student days, combine to make a picture which many a listener has registered with happy admiration; but those same listeners will be aware that the reason why they have wanted to hear this man preach again had to do with something vastly deeper. They could not long be conscious of outward aspects when the man was so completely unconscious of himself, and so caught up in the larger Reality that possessed him. If they sought for words to describe what they felt about him they might well have repeated what the crowd in Capernaum said of the Christian preachers' Master: "He taught with authority and not as the scribes." For when this man speaks of God and for God, there is no echoing of second-hand traditions. There is the ring of unhesitant conviction which carries authentic power.[5]

Think of that: the "authentic power" of the sermon because of the "larger Reality that possessed him." He speaks "of God and for God" because he knows God whose Word has worked for him and now works through him.

Before we preach a sermon we must ask ourselves "Is this true for me? Have I firsthand knowledge of it? Am I sure of it?" Of course, there will be heights and depths of the Word we have neither scaled nor plumbed; if we talk of them we must do so as sinners

[5] Walter Russell Bowie in *This Ministry: The Contribution of Henry Sloane Coffin* (New York: Charles Scribner's Sons, 1945), pp. 59-60.

and as searchers. Yet *the* Word must become *my* Word, not in the sense that I have taken possession of it, but with the significance that it has laid hold on me. When it has possessed me, then I am ready to share it.

Such a man is not only entitled to tell others about the things of God, he must. There is an inner compulsion which constrains him. His preaching will be aimed at turning the hearer into a believer, the believer into a disciple, and the disciple into an apostle. It is wise for us who are in the pulpit to remember that there are believers and apostles in the pew. They, too, are re-incarnations of the Word. God does not commit His good news only to professionals. Let us look now, in appreciation, at the layman who is a believer.

Romans 16:1-16, in the Moffatt translation is fast becoming one of my favorite chapters in the Bible. In it Paul is saying: "Thank you. Thank you very much" to a group of first-century Christians. He has finished with arguing and exhorting, with haranguing and debating. He is just remembering a group of men and women in the church and being grateful to them out loud. Whom is he thanking? There are folk like Priscilla and Aquila, a husband and wife to whom Paul was devoted. He says they had risked their lives for him, and he wants to convey the gratitude of the Gentile churches as well as his own to them (verses 3-4). We learn elsewhere that they had once straightened out a preacher on his doctrine (Acts 19:24-28)! Then there were Andronicus and Junias. Paul says they were Jews who had been incarcerated with him (verse 7). Think of the status accorded a man who could say that he and Paul had been in jail together at Caesarea or Ephesus or Rome. Talk about the old school tie! Three women are mentioned together, Tryphena, Tryphosa, and Persis "who [have] worked very hard in the Lord" (verse 12). Next time someone says to you that Paul had a low estimate of women read that verse to him. Of course, Paul was not always consistent in his opinion of the other sex; that just proves he was a man. But in this chapter, in this verse and elsewhere, he shows his appreciation of their work for Christ. Do you grasp why I love this chapter? Because it tells me that the Pauls and the Peters could not have done the kind of work they did for God if Andronicus and Junias and Tryphena and Tryphosa had not been holding up their hands. It reminds me, as an ordained clergyman, of the consecrated work of the ordinary churchmen and churchwomen who are, as I am, believers in the Word of God and, maybe better than I am, doers of it.

I told you about two men being fellow prisoners of Paul. There is something else in that verse that every young clergyman should remember as he prepares his sermons and visits his parishioners. Paul says about Andronicus and Junias very simply and, I believe, very humbly: "They were in Christ before me." We never hear of them anywhere else in the New Testament though they were "men of note among the Apostles." But they were in Christ longer than Paul. We are going to find them in our parishes, the old Christians, of both sexes, who gave themselves to Christ and to his God before we did. The thought humbles one, and there is no harm in that. Therefore, sit at their feet when you visit them; ask them to pray with you and for you; give thanks to God that they are not only your flock but also your shepherds.

For they are still with us. Their name is legion, and they come from all classes and walks in life. Offhand, I can think of a Philadelphia lawyer, a school carpenter, a dining room steward, a housewife, a paper hanger, a commercial traveler, a middle-aged widow, a surgeon and a school teacher who are of their number. We do not have to convert them; they are already believers. But, because of our training, we may be able to help them to a fuller knowledge of the Christian World-view. That is why regular pastoral preaching must be teaching (*didaché*) as well as proclamation (*kerygma*). In the pulpits of our parishes I would say that it ought to be primarily teaching, the explication of the proclamation, so that it may be understood and practiced in the personal and social lives of the believers.

Before I leave the layman let me stress again that we can learn from him about the things of God. He may help us to understand the Word of God as he has been privileged to know it. In this connection I think of a general practitioner with whom I served in a medical panel on "The Care of the Terminal Patient." He told the students present that when they dealt with people in the final stages of illness, the job to be done was to walk with the patient through the valley of the shadow of death—not just *in* it, but *through* it. The Old Testament department may shake its head at such an exegesis of the twenty-third Psalm, but spiritually the general practitioner is right. Do you know how I know he is right? Because he does just that. He has walked with many a patient in the valley, brought him through it, and then returned to tell those who mourn that all is well. When I preach I try to remember those who are "farther ben" in the things of Christ than I am.

*   *   *   *   *   *

What kind of life does the believer live now that he is an agent of the Word in the ministry of reconciliation? It is one of daily commuting between the Church and the World. We know what the World is:

society organized without much, if any, reference to God. In that kind of a World the lay believer has to earn his bread. But what is the Church? Paul has a name for the Church in his letter to a little group of believers in Philippi. Dr. Moffatt paraphrases the Greek words thus:

We are a colony of heaven.   (PHILIPPIANS 3:20)

What was Paul thinking about when he used such a metaphor? Remember that he was a Roman citizen, and glad of it; he used the fact to his own advantage more than once. Now the Romans were colonists. What was a Roman colony? It was, originally, a group of army veterans and their families set down in an outpost in the midst of hostile territory, miles from the mother country. That was a situation which called for vigilance without and comradeship within. Inside the colony the laws of Rome were in operation. The spirit of Rome was there, transplanted from overseas.

Philippi was a Roman colony, a miniature Rome in northern Greece. Its inhabitants, who were members of the local church, would know what Paul was suggesting when he wrote: "We are a colony of heaven." They would understand his analogy. Their little church was a colony of the Kingdom of God. It was not the mother country, but the rules of the homeland were in operation within this Christian outpost. For the believer today, as for the Philippians, the Church is a colony of heaven set down in the World. The believer may work in the World, but he should not be entirely at home there. The Church is the dwelling place of his spirit which knows that its real citizenship is in Heaven. Thus there is always an antagonism between the Church and the World. This is inevitable by definition: one is organized around God, the other apart from God. Even when there is but little patent hostility there should be obvious signs of a cold war. What the Christian must fear is a working alliance or even a friendly truce between the Church and the World.

Therefore, for the believer, the Church has a two-fold significance. First of all, it is a place of withdrawal from the World, for worship. Worship is the appreciation of the worth-while fact of God and of His saving Word. The Church exists to celebrate that fact, to understand it and to proclaim it. Here the believer, in joyous company with like-minded brethren, focuses his heart and mind on God. The first note of worship is one of adoration. It is immediately followed by the recognition that one has but little right to place himself in the presence of God, because of one's creaturehood and one's sin. Again, almost immediately, that is followed by the

remembrance of the gracious Word of God which recon-
ciles the worshipper to God, so that thanksgiving is the
inevitable response. Adoration, confession, forgiveness
and thanksgiving together make up the first act in worship, private or public, individual or corporate. The
Church reminds the believer of the fact which the World
wishes him to forget or to deny: that God is, and is
supreme, and is favorable to man.

Because the believer is not alone he must have some
sort of an attitude toward his fellow worshippers. That
is determined for him: He must treat them as God treated
him. Remembering this he acts in love. Christian love
is not in essence an emotional response of the heart, but
the steady, intelligent outgoing of the whole man in
good will toward his fellow colonists. In worship he
never forgets the prayer of intercession and the acts of
love which flow from it.

So that he may be constantly reminded of the World-
view of his faith, the Bible must be heard, and ex-
pounded, and applied. Hence, the importance of the
reading and the preaching of the Word. This will be
supplemented by Sunday school and Bible class, whose
primary purpose will be what "school" and "class"
suggest: a serious, consecutive, organized study of the
Word of God.

In addition to being a place of withdrawal, the

Church as a colony is also a place of return to the World, for witness. Fortified by his contact with God and informed by his study of the Word, he is ready to be known as a citizen of the Kingdom. His behavior ought to give him away. It is said that Tertullian became a Christian, not because of any rational arguments in its favor, but because he was inspired by the behavior of some Christian slaves in the market place. A Christian will be known often by the way in which he does very simple things. It may be the tone of his voice as he excuses the clumsiness of a restless straphanger. It may be the sparkle in his eye as he offers to carry a bag in a crowded railroad station. It may be the sense of humor which can make him laugh at himself as his personal dignity is imperilled. It may be the unusual common sense which makes him realize that there are times when a pipeline of cold water is a more Christian solution to corporate thirst than a cup of cold water. Such a believer realizes that there is only one Gospel, but that there may be two ways of applying it, the personal and the social. Therefore, he works willingly, as a Christian, on the Community Chest. He may even, as a Christian, run for political office, if it is for him the wisest way of expressing his Christian love. He knows that the willingly accepted duty laid on him is that he must witness in the World.

If the believer chooses either withdrawal or witness by itself, without reference to the other, then he is an incomplete Christian. There have been those who in despair of the World live only in the colony, and even narrow its activities to attendance at services where no sermon is preached. (A rector had better examine himself and his flock if the best attended service is at eight o'clock on Sunday morning.) What shall we say to these resigned heretics whose theme song is: "Sit down, O men of God"? Remind them of Jesus, who preferred the bustle of Galilee to the monastic retreats of Trans-Jordan; whose highest compliment was paid to a Roman officer; whose most attractive hero was a despised Samaritan; whose friends were the outcasts of Israel. He worked in the World. No colony of the Kingdom should ever be called "The Church of the Heavenly Rest." The colony is the Church militant, not triumphant—and not dormant. The Church is for withdrawal, not for escape. It is for refurbishing, renewal and reconsecration so that one may return to witness in the World.

There have been those who sought in enthusiastic witness to build the Kingdom of God on earth. More than anyone else we Americans are accused of seeking to erect the New Jerusalem on top of the cities and villages already established. Some of us do not pray that God's Kingdom may come; we offer to draw the blueprints and set about construction. We grow tired of ritual and form, of praise and prayer; we want to make man good and life abundant by higher wages and shorter hours and government housing, all effected through legislation. What shall be said to this kind of enthusiast? Perhaps he should be reminded that our job is not to build the Kingdom but to witness to it; that the Kingdom is a gift from God and not an achievement of man.

The believer refuses the alternative, withdrawal or witness; he chooses both. Thus he escapes from the debilitating mistake of thinking he is already in the mother country while he is actually on duty in the colony. He knows that there is business to be done in the World. He also escapes the wearied cynicism or disappointed frustration of the tired radical who has discovered that he cannot build the Kingdom. The believer knows that, while he is on earth, the Church is all the Kingdom he will know. He will accept it as a colony and try to purify its life, by prayer and deed, so that it may be worthy of the homeland. If it is a good colony other men of the World may be tempted to become members of it.

The believer walks in the World as a sympathetic stranger in an alien land where perforce he must spend much of his time on earth. But he knows that the World is not for him. He is ready to help its inhabitants in love; he must, because of his new nature. He does not expect to effect much more than temporary amelioration or partial improvement. Thus he is not too disappointed when goals are not reached or ideals are compromised. He will continue to give cups of cold water or build pipelines of cold water. He will continue to speak a word in private or make a speech in a legislature. Why? Because he wishes and wills to continue his Christian witness, in success and in failure. For him success and failure are but by-products, the real job is witness. In that he has his joy. He sows as well as he can; maybe God will give the increase; that is His responsibility. Thus he works with the strain off. It is sometimes wise to remember that there is such a thing as Christian nonchalance. Maybe there is room for a new beatitude: "Blessed are the debonair," in whom the Word of God sparkles with graciousness and charm.

It is that kind of believer whom our sermons are supposed to create and establish.

In Conclusion

WHEN a monarch [1] is crowned in Westminster Abbey, the Archbishop of Canterbury, receiving the Bible from off the altar, gives it to the sovereign saying: "Our gracious King, we present you with this Book, the most valuable thing that this world affords. Here is wisdom; this is the royal Law; these are the lively Oracles of God." We have sought in this book to appreciate the statement that the Bible is "the most valuable thing that this world (with a small 'w'!) affords." We know that it is the vehicle of the Word of God.

To us is given the task of expounding this Word. That is an awesome responsibility. It has been brought home to me with seriousness by some lines of Shakespeare. Prince John of Lancaster is addressing the Arch-

---

[1] At the Coronation of Queen Elizabeth II the Bible was presented to the Queen by the Moderator of the General Assembly of the Church of Scotland.

bishop of York, whom he has reprimanded for bearing arms against the King. There may be sarcasm in his tone, but he puts his finger on what the man in the pulpit should be and do:

> Who hath not heard it spoken
> How deep you were within the books of God?
> To us the speaker in his parliament;
> To us the imagined voice of God himself;
> The very opener and intelligencer
> Between the grace, the sanctities of heaven
> And our dull workings.
>
> (KING HENRY IV—Part II, Act iv, Sc. 2)

"Deep within the books of God" so that we become "the imagined voice of God himself." How dare any man seek to attain such a position? He may dare only if he does so, to use the words of Bacon, "for the glory of the Creator and the relief of man's estate."

Index